Peterson Institute for International Economics

World on the Move

Consumption Patterns in a More Equal Global Economy

POLICY ANALYSES IN INTERNATIONAL ECONOMICS 105

Peterson Institute for International Economics

World on the Move

Consumption Patterns in a More Equal Global Economy

POLICY ANALYSES IN INTERNATIONAL ECONOMICS 105

Tomáš Hellebrandt and Paolo Mauro
Assisted by Ján Žilinský

Washington, DC
December 2016

Tomáš Hellebrandt was research fellow at the Peterson Institute for International Economics from 2013 to 2015. Before that he was an economist at the Bank of England from 2007 to 2013. He is the author of "Income Inequality Developments in the Great Recession" (PIIE Policy Brief, January 2014).

Paolo Mauro is assistant director in the African Department of the International Monetary Fund (IMF). He was senior fellow at the Peterson Institute for International Economics and visiting professor at the Johns Hopkins University Carey Business School in 2014–16. Before that he held various managerial positions in the IMF's research and fiscal affairs departments. His articles have been published in journals including the *Quarterly Journal of Economics* and have been highly cited in academia and leading media outlets such as the *Economist* and *Wall Street Journal.* His previous books are *Emerging Markets and Financial Globalization* (Oxford University Press, 2007) and *Chipping Away at Public Debt* (Wiley, 2011).

**PETERSON INSTITUTE FOR
INTERNATIONAL ECONOMICS**
1750 Massachusetts Avenue, NW
Washington, DC 20036-1903
(202) 328-9000   FAX: (202) 328-5432
www.piie.com

Adam S. Posen, *President*
Steven R. Weisman, *Vice President for
Publications and Communications*

Cover Design by Fletcher Design, Inc.—
Washington, DC
Cover Photo by ©naveen0301—iStock
Printing by Versa Press, Inc.

Printed in the United States of America
18   17   16   5   4   3   2   1

**Library of Congress
Cataloging-in-Publication Data**
Names: Hellebrandt, Tomáš, author. | Mauro, Paolo, author. Title: World on the move : consumption patterns in a more equal global economy / Tomáš Hellebrandt and Paolo Mauro. Description: Washington, DC : Peterson Institute for International Economics, 2016. | Includes bibliographical references. Identifiers: LCCN 2016027392 (print) | LCCN 2016040777 (ebook) | ISBN 9780881327168 | ISBN 9780881327175 Subjects: LCSH: Income distribution. | Consumption (Economics) | Population— Economic aspects. | Globalization—Economic aspects. Classification: LCC HC79.I5 H45 2016 (print) | LCC HC79.I5 (ebook) | DDC 339.2—dc23 LC record available at https://lccn.loc.gov/2016027392

*This publication has been subjected to a prepublication peer review intended to ensure analytical quality. The views expressed are those of the authors. This publication is part of the overall program of the Peterson Institute for International Economics, as endorsed by its Board of Directors, but it does not necessarily reflect the views of individual members of the Board or of the Institute's staff or management.
The Peterson Institute for International Economics is a private nonpartisan, nonprofit institution for rigorous, intellectually open, and indepth study and discussion of international economic policy. Its purpose is to identify and analyze important issues to make globalization beneficial and sustainable for the people of the United States and the world, and then to develop and communicate practical new approaches for dealing with them.
Its work is funded by a highly diverse group of philanthropic foundations, private corporations, and interested individuals, as well as income on its capital fund. About 35 percent of the Institute's resources in its latest fiscal year were provided by contributors from outside the United States. A list of all financial supporters for the preceding six years is posted at https://piie.com/sites/default/files/supporters.pdf.*

Contents

Figures

Preface

The public discourse about inequality in the United States and some other advanced economies is understandably dominated by concerns about the rising income share of a relatively few rich individuals relative to the vast majority of working families. Yet in a historic shift, growing incomes in emerging markets are allowing hundreds of millions of people to join the consumer class. Ignoring national borders, individual incomes of the entire world's population are becoming more, not less, equal. Beginning around the turn of this century, global inequality has gradually declined for the first time since today's advanced economies pulled ahead of the rest of the world during the Industrial Revolution. In this study, Tomáš Hellebrandt and Paolo Mauro painstakingly combine consensus forecasts of the long-term growth of output and population with detailed information on the distribution of incomes and consumption from surveys of thousands of households worldwide to show that, under reasonable assumptions, this hopeful trend will continue during the next two decades.

How incomes are distributed among the world's citizens matters for the types of good and services people will buy, because spending choices depend on income levels. People are becoming more equal not only in incomes but also in the items they spend on, as emerging-market economy residents are increasingly able to afford goods and services previously available only to rich-country residents. Using the projected global distribution of incomes as a stepping stone, and novel estimates of the link between individual incomes and consumption of items such as food and transportation, the authors project what people will spend on twenty years from now.

They find, notably, that expenditure on transportation will rise fourfold in China, India, and Sub-Saharan Africa. These are exciting developments: Greater consumption indicates rising well-being and provides opportunities for businesses and investors located not only in emerging markets, but also in advanced economies.

For this scenario to occur, however, the necessary investment in infrastructure in many emerging-market economies such as India will be massive. By drawing on information about the distribution of individual incomes, Hellebrandt and Mauro find larger investment needs than previous studies. Beyond mobilizing their own fiscal resources, governments will need to attract financing from the private sector on an unprecedented scale. The authors also show that investment needs are greatest in countries with weak institutions, so they offer suggestions to enhance transparency and strengthen budgetary processes to ensure both that public money is not wasted and that the public sector is not saddled with fiscal risks from excessive guarantees to private providers.

Moreover, rising consumption on the projected scale will put strains on natural resources and the climate. Malthusian doomsday scenarios have previously proven unwarranted, as human ingenuity and private profit incentives have made it possible to increase productivity. But this time may be different, because climate change causes powerful international spillovers. Global cooperation will be key to avoiding catastrophe, and the authors point to priority areas of expenditure in that regard.

This book takes a further step in the Institute's well-established line of research on inequality and long-run growth from a global perspective, building on recent books by Caroline Freund on emerging-market billionaires (*Rich People, Poor Countries: The Rise of Emerging-Market Tycoons and Their Mega Firms*), Arvind Subramanian (*Eclipse: Living in the Shadow of China's Economic Dominance*), and many other PIIE researchers, as well as Surjit Bhalla's 2002 Institute volume, *Imagine There's No Country: Poverty, Inequality, and Growth in the Era of Globalization*.

The Peterson Institute for International Economics is a private nonpartisan, nonprofit institution for rigorous, intellectually open, and in-depth study and discussion of international economic policy. Its purpose is to identify and analyze important issues to making globalization beneficial and sustainable for the people of the United States and the world, and then to develop and communicate practical new approaches for dealing with them.

The Institute's work is funded by a highly diverse group of philanthropic foundations, private corporations, public institutions, and interested individuals, as well as by income on its capital fund. About 35 percent of the Institute's resources in our latest fiscal year were provided by contributors from outside the United States. The production of this book is partially supported by a generous grant from the GE Foundation. A list of all our financial supporters for the preceding year is posted at https://piie.com/sites/default/files/supporters.pdf.

The Executive Committee of the Institute's Board of Directors bears overall responsibility for the Institute's direction, gives general guidance and approval to its research program, and evaluates its performance in pursuit of its mission. The Institute's President is responsible for the identification of topics that are likely to become important over the medium term (one to three years) that should be addressed by Institute scholars. This rolling agenda is set in close consultation with the Institute's research staff, Board of Directors, and other stakeholders.

The President makes the final decision to publish any individual Institute study, following independent internal and external review of the work. Interested readers may access the data and computations underlying the Institute publications for research and replication by searching titles at www.piie.com.

The Institute hopes that its research and other activities will contribute to building a stronger foundation for international economic policy around the world. We invite readers of these publications to let us know how they think we can best accomplish this objective.

ADAM S. POSEN
President
November 2016

Acknowledgments

We are grateful to Ján Žilinský, whose excellent econometric and programming skills were instrumental to the completion of this highly data-intensive project.

Olivier Dupriez shared expertise and data on household surveys of consumption. William R. Cline, Pedro Nicolaci da Costa, Rob Dellink, Andrew Mason, Marcus Noland, Adam S. Posen, David J. Stockton, Edwin M. Truman, Steven R. Weisman, and Ján Žilinský provided insightful and detailed comments. We received helpful suggestions from Bertrand Badré, Olivier Blanchard, Marianne Fay, Caroline Freund, Joseph Gagnon, Nicholas R. Lardy, Branko Milanović, Abebe A. Selassie, Andy Sumner, and Nicolas Véron.

We also benefited from suggestions received at seminars at the International Finance Corporation, the International Monetary Fund's Fiscal Affairs Department, the Johns Hopkins University Carey Business School, and the US Treasury, at conferences organized by CF40-PIIE in Beijing, Banco de Guatemala in Guatemala City, and the World Bank's Chief Economist Office in Delhi, as well as a study group at PIIE and a presentation to the PIIE Board of Directors meeting.

We thank PIIE President Adam Posen for encouraging us from the inception of the project and providing guidance and support throughout its implementation. We are also grateful to Steven R. Weisman for overseeing the publications team, to Madona Devasahayam, Barbara Karni, and Susann Luetjen for excellent editorial and publishing assistance, and to Egor Gornostay for verifying and reproducing our results.

The GE Foundation provided generous financial support and the ERANDA Foundation generously supported this project through a grant to the Institute for work on inequality and inclusive capitalism.

The Changing Landscape of Global Consumption

"Do you need one burner or two in your stove?" asks the salesman. Grace Makutsi, a graduate of the Botswana College of Business and Secretarial School, hesitates for a moment. She and her husband are choosing appliances for the modest house they just purchased. Never in her wildest dreams had she imagined she would be in a position to have a stove with two burners. She delights in the prospect and feels proud of her achievements.

Balram Halwai is the son of a rickshaw puller in rural India and has worked his way up to become the main driver of a local landlord. Through wit and ruthlessness, he has mustered the resources to acquire his own taxi company in Bangalore. When boasting about his material success, he points to his ownership of a chandelier and a laptop.

Makutsi and Halwai—fictional characters from bestsellers[1]—live continents apart and have very different lives. But they share a sense of enthusiasm about modern consumer goods that are taken for granted in the rich world, as well as a feeling of accomplishment in having acquired them.

Nearly a billion people in emerging-market economies in Asia and Sub-Saharan Africa will join the modern consumer classes over the next two decades.[2] Rising incomes will enable them to buy adequate food and simple goods such as toothpaste, bicycles, and television sets for the first time. Meanwhile, hundreds of millions of people who now live modestly

---

1. Alexander McCall Smith's *The Limpopo Academy of Private Detection* (2013) and Aravind Adiga's *The White Tiger* (2008).

2. Throughout the book, the term "emerging-market economies" includes all nonadvanced economies.

will be able to purchase cars, air tickets, and improved medical care. The unprecedented demographic boom in Sub-Saharan Africa and continued rapid population growth in India—as population stagnates in China and most advanced economies—will shift the world's economic center of gravity toward consumers in emerging-market Asia and, to some extent, Sub-Saharan Africa, offering fresh opportunities to companies and investors. Firms in these markets will become more productive by adopting modern technology and business practices and adapting them to local conditions. Output will increase, further raising the incomes and spending of the residents of emerging-market economies.

Focus of the Book

To better understand these trends and their policy implications, this book focuses on people rather than countries. Instead of relying solely on macroeconomic statistics, such as per capita GDP, it uses household surveys, in which thousands of people representative of a country's population provide information on their incomes and spending by category. Each country's household survey reveals the number of people who earn a given income level and what they spend their money on. Combining this information with forecasts of output and population for each country, the book projects the global distribution of individual incomes and consumption 20 years from now. It then uses the projected global income distribution to forecast what categories of goods and services will be in greatest demand and in which regions in the next two decades.

How future global gains in income are distributed among the world's citizens is important not only in its own right but also because it affects the types of goods and services people will buy. If all income gains were to accrue to the richest people on the planet, spending on sports cars and luxury handbags would rise, but demand for wheat and soap would remain unchanged. In contrast, if the gains were to accrue to the poorest people, spending on food and other basic necessities would rise significantly.

The analysis in this book reveals not only that global income inequality will decline but also that hundreds of millions of people worldwide will be able to afford the goods and services that until recently have been widely consumed only in advanced economies. In that broad sense, the world's citizens are projected to become more equal in terms of what they consume as well.[3] As the income gap between the global rich (mostly residents of

---

3. This book does not examine the extent to which closing income and consumption gaps will result in lower disparities in perceived well-being, happiness, or health outcomes. On the relationship between income, consumption, and those outcomes, see Deaton (2013).

advanced economies) and the rest narrows, spending on transportation will rise dramatically. The increase will require massive investments in infrastructure (railways, bridges, roads, and ports), putting strains on government budgets, scarce natural resources, and the environment. Rising consumption of meat and fish could also have ominous implications for land, water, and ocean resources as well as for the climate.[4]

This analysis focuses on income and consumption rather than wealth for several reasons. First, data on income and consumption are more generally available and allow for more sophisticated analysis.[5] Second, as the bottom half of the world's population has long had essentially no wealth, trends in indicators such as the number of billionaires (who have as much wealth as the bottom half of the world's population) or the wealth held by the top 1 or 50 percent would not be as informative as trends in the incomes of the corresponding shares. Third, income is more relevant than wealth in forecasting what people—especially people in the bottom half of the distribution—will buy.[6]

Key Findings

Ignoring national borders, the distribution of individual incomes of all people worldwide will become more equal in the next 20 years. Rising incomes in emerging-market economies will increase spending on transportation, which will require enormous infrastructure investment in these countries. Government processes will have to become more transparent to ensure that the money is not wasted on unnecessary or poorly implemented projects.

Global Income Distribution

For the first time since the Industrial Revolution allowed today's advanced economies to pull away from the rest of the world and deliver unprecedented levels of affluence to their citizens, the gap between the global rich

---

4. Compared with vegetarian sources of calories and protein, meat requires more water and energy to produce and leads to higher greenhouse emissions (Foley 2014, Kunzig 2014).

5. The best data on the global wealth distribution were assembled and analyzed by Davies et al. (2011) and partially updated and popularized by Credit Suisse (2014) and Oxfam (2016). According to Oxfam, the net wealth of the world's wealthiest 60 individuals is as great as that of the bottom 50 percent of the world's population.

6. Although income is more relevant for projecting expenditures, wealth (which is distributed more unequally than income) is also an important measure. The lack of wealth leaves people at the bottom of the distribution highly vulnerable: With no assets to tap during bad times, they are unable to smooth their consumption and are thus wholly exposed to the vagaries of their incomes.

and the global poor started declining significantly at the turn of the 21st century. This trend of falling global inequality is expected to continue for the next two decades, under the economics profession's consensus projections for output and population growth in individual countries.

In the baseline scenario, the Gini index for worldwide income distribution is projected to decline from 69.1 in 2015 to 66.6 in 2035.[7] (It was 73.8 in 2003 and at similar values in the late 1980s.) In 2015 the global income of individuals in the 90th percentile of the income distribution was 29 times that of people in the 10th percentile.[8] This ratio is projected to fall to 25 in 2035, primarily as a result of faster economic growth in emerging-market economies than in advanced economies. Rising incomes in emerging-market economies are expected to lift almost half a billion people out of extreme poverty, defined as living on less than $1.90 a day.

If income inequality within countries evolves with economic growth based on the relationship between inequality and affluence observed across countries, global inequality could fall even faster. In this scenario the global Gini index would reach 63.0 in 2035. Under an alternative, more pessimistic scenario—in which countries' economic growth rates gradually revert to the worldwide average growth rate observed over the past 50 years, reducing the pace of convergence between emerging-market and advanced economies—inequality declines more slowly, with the Gini index reaching 68.2 in 2035.

Under the baseline scenario, the global pool of consumers will increase, with the largest net gains in emerging-market economies. The number of people with annual household incomes below $2,000 (in international US dollars at 2011 prices) is projected to decline by more than 1.1 billion.[9] The $2,000–$6,000 income bracket will swell by about 700 million people, with the largest gains in Sub-Saharan Africa and India. The number of people

---

7. The Gini index (or coefficient) is the most common indicator of inequality. It ranges from 0 (a situation in which everyone in the economy has the same income) to 100 (a situation in which a single person in the economy earns all the income).

8. In a population of 100 people ranked by ascending order of income, the 90th percentile would represent the income of person number 90 (i.e., the person with the 10th-highest income). The ratio of the 90th to the 10th percentile is a common way of summarizing income inequality that reduces the influence of extreme poverty and extreme affluence.

9. Throughout this book, data are presented in constant 2011 prices in international US dollars. Data in local currency are converted to international US dollars using purchasing power parity exchange rates drawn from the World Bank's *World Development Indicators*. Such exchange rates measure the relative cost of purchasing the same basket of consumer goods and services in different countries. They take into consideration the fact that, for example, the price of a haircut is cheaper in an emerging-market economy than in the United States.

with incomes of $6,000–$20,000 will increase by a little over a billion, with the largest gains in India and China. The number of people with incomes over $20,000 will increase by almost 800 million, with the largest gains in the advanced economies and China.

Global Consumption Patterns

As incomes rise, people across cultures increase their spending on transportation more than proportionately. Growth of transportation spending will be especially strong in emerging-market Asia—including China and India—and Sub-Saharan Africa, where large segments of the population are on the cusp of being able to afford cars and air travel for the first time. Spending on transportation will increase well in excess of total consumption in most emerging-market economies. It is projected to increase by a factor of four in India, followed closely by China and Sub-Saharan Africa; three or more in East Asia and the Pacific; and at least two in all remaining emerging-market regions. Global spending on transportation is projected to increase by 127 percent between 2015 and 2035, compared with 107 percent for total consumption. The global difference is more modest than regional differences, because much of today's transportation spending occurs in advanced economies, where spending is projected to grow relatively slowly in the next two decades.

Food consumption will rise more slowly than household incomes, as people divert some of their resources to nonessential items. The highest growth rate is projected in Sub-Saharan Africa (145 percent), in part because of the rapid growth of total consumption there (the gap between the growth rates of food consumption and total consumption is relatively small because of the sizable initial share of food in total consumption in Sub-Saharan Africa). India will also see food consumption at least double (110 percent growth); Southeast Asia, East Asia and the Pacific, and China will see growth of 80–90 percent. The lowest growth rates for food spending (about 30 percent) are projected in the countries of the European Union and the Organization for Economic Cooperation and Development, Eastern Europe, and Central Asia.

Food consumption is projected to grow more slowly than total consumption, but the increase will still put considerable pressure on natural resources. As individual incomes rise from very low levels, consumers usually increase the share of meat and fish in their diets.[10]

---

10. For example, daily consumption of animal source foodstuffs (measured in grams per capita) in China is twice as large for high-income households as for low-income households (Du et al. 2004).

Infrastructure Needs

The projected shift in spending patterns over the next 20 years—which will disproportionately benefit people in emerging-market economies—means that more infrastructure will be needed than would be projected on the basis of GDP growth alone. Just building new paved roads and railroads will cost an estimated $48 trillion through 2035, according to this book's analysis.

The needs are so massive that governments will not be able to act alone; the private sector will need to participate on a grand scale. Transparency will be needed in dealings with private sector actors, to ensure that they—and government officials—do not profit unfairly, by overbilling, delivering substandard products, or building unnecessary projects. The potential for corruption is enormous, especially because needs will be greatest in many of the countries in which governance is weak.

To finance these expenses—as well as the costs of maintaining this infrastructure—governments will need to start making decisions about tax and expenditure policies soon. They will also need to choose options that are climate-friendly (building metros and railways rather than roads, for example, and investing in renewable energy rather than coal). Given the long lives of infrastructure, choices made today will affect the livability of emerging-market megacities and the global climate for generations.

2

Projecting Growth in Populations and Incomes

Prediction is very difficult, especially if it's about the future.
—Danish proverb, sometimes
attributed to Niels Bohr

Projecting the global distribution of individual incomes 20 years into the future requires making assumptions about the evolution of populations, incomes, and the distribution of those incomes among residents of every country in the world. This chapter reports the projections of population and GDP by demographers and economists. Chapter 3 examines income distribution within countries.

Estimates and Projections of Population and Income

The analysis first reports forecasts from international institutions, academics, and private sector forecasters (appendix 2A provides detail). It then uses those forecasts to project the global income distribution and resulting consumption patterns in later chapters.

Population Growth

The world's population is projected to rise from about 7.3 billion in 2015 to about 8.8 billion in 2035. Most of the increase will be in emerging-market economies (figure 2.1). Sub-Saharan Africa will see the largest increase, growing from a little below 1 billion to nearly 1.6 billion. India's population will rise by 270 million, overtaking China as the world's most populous country in 2022. The population will also increase significantly in parts of South and East Asia, Latin America and the Caribbean, and the Middle East and North Africa.

Figure 2.1 Estimated (2015) and projected (2035) world population

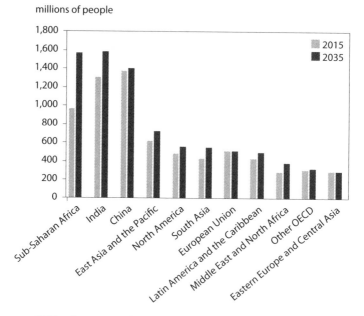

millions of people

OECD = Organization for Economic Cooperation and Development
Note: The sample is restricted to countries with more than 1 million inhabitants and for which inequality data are available.
Source: United Nations (2015).

The largest percentage increase will be in Sub-Saharan Africa, where the share of the world's population will rise from 13 percent in 2015 to 18 percent in 2035. Rapid population growth in Sub-Saharan Africa is projected to continue well into the late 21st century—Africa accounts for 3.2 billion of the projected 4 billion increase in the global population by 2100 (Drummond, Thakoor, and Yu 2014)—leading some observers to refer to the "African Century."[1] Africa's working-age (15–64) population is projected to rise by 2.1 billion—exceeding the net global increase of 2 billion. Its share of the global working-age population is projected to increase from less than 13 percent in 2010 to more than 41 percent by 2100 (United Nations 2015). These developments will be transformational for Africa and will have major effects on the global economy.

In contrast, the population will remain flat in Eastern Europe and

---

1. Antoinette M. Sayeh and Abebe A. Selassie, "The African Century," iMFdirect blog, August 3, 2015, International Monetary Fund, http://blog-imfdirect.imf.org/2015/08/03/the-african-century.

Central Asia and increase only modestly in China.[2] It will grow slowly in the advanced economies, with net gains only in the United States, Australia, and Canada. As a result, the advanced economies' share of the world's population will decline, from 15 percent in 2015 to 13 percent in 2035.

Growth of Per Capita and Total Incomes

Annual average per capita GDP growth in 2015–35 is projected to be higher in emerging-market economies (3.4 percent) than in advanced economies (2 percent). It will be strong not only in China (4.2 percent) and India (4.7 percent) but also in Sub-Saharan Africa (3.3 percent). Total GDP growth is projected to be highest in Sub-Saharan Africa (5.8 percent) and India (5.7 percent), reflecting rapid growth in both population and per capita incomes (figure 2.2). China's per capita income growth is projected to remain among the fastest, but its low population growth implies that its total GDP growth will lag behind some of the other emerging-market economies.

By 2035 the share of emerging-market economies in total real output will reach 66 percent, up from 56 percent in 2015. The largest economies are projected to be China (with 21 percent of the world's GDP), the United States (with 14 percent), and India (with 11 percent) (see figure 2.3).

Size of the Global Economy and Per Capita GDP

Global GDP was $107.2 trillion in 2015 in purchasing power parity terms, according to the World Bank's *World Development Indicators*, which collects data on 186 countries. Combining this figure with the individual country projections for population and output per capita reported above yields projected global GDP of $213 trillion by 2035, or an average annual GDP growth rate of 3.5 percent over the next two decades. The medium-fertility scenario projections of the United Nations indicate a global population of 8.84 billion people in 2035 (an average increase of 0.9 percent a year). Per capita GDP worldwide is thus projected to rise from $14,588 in 2015 to $24,624 in 2035, an average annual real per capita increase of 2.7 percent over 20 years.

---

2. The population projections used in this book were issued by the United Nations before China lifted its one-child policy (in late October 2015). Demographers believe that the shift is unlikely to have a major impact on fertility rates or speed up population growth substantially, particularly over the next two decades (Schiermeier 2015).

Figure 2.2 Projected average annual per capita and total GDP growth rates between 2015 and 2035, by region

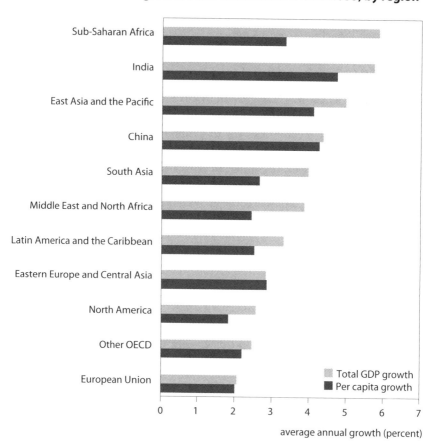

OECD = Organization for Economic Cooperation and Development

Note: The sample is restricted to countries with more than 1 million inhabitants and for which inequality data are available.

Source: See appendix table 2A.2.

Reliability of Long-Run Projections of Economic Growth and Population

The ability to forecast GDP growth accurately beyond the next year or so is limited; economic projections about 2035 are thus highly uncertain. Making projections is nevertheless important, because decisions by policy-makers as well as business executives and investors need to be based on informed guesses about future economic developments.

Most economists agree that economic growth in the advanced economies over the next decade is likely to moderate, although there is debate

Figure 2.3 Estimated (2015) and projected (2035) country and regional shares of total GDP

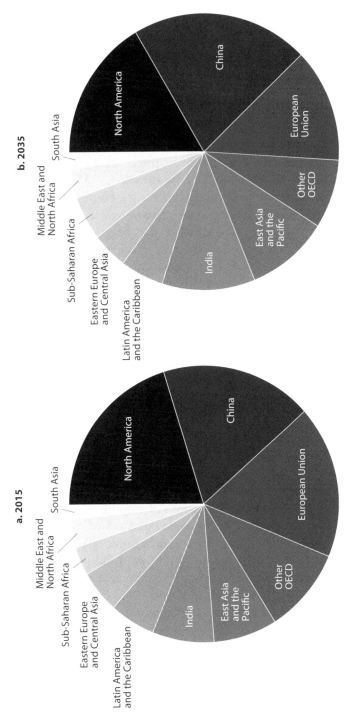

a. 2015

b. 2035

OECD = Organization for Economic Cooperation and Development

Note: The sample is restricted to countries with more than 1 million inhabitants and for which inequality data are available.

Sources: See appendix table 2A.2.

over the reasons for the slowdown. Some argue that the world economy is experiencing "secular stagnation"—prolonged weak economic growth caused by low investment demand and overabundant savings (Summers 2016). Others argue that technology could slow growth. Robert Gordon (2015) suggests that the world is unlikely to see innovations that are as life altering as those invented between 1870 and 1970 and that the current generation of young people may be the first in US history whose living standards fail to exceed those of their parents. On the other side are economists such as Joel Mokyr, Chris Vickers, and Nicolas L. Ziebrath (2015), who point to a long history of pessimistic predictions about the inevitable limits of technological progress that have turned out to be unfounded.

The projections used in this book reflect the consensus among economists that the long-run economic growth rate is likely to be lower than before the economic and financial crisis that began in 2008. Emerging-market economies are projected to grow more rapidly than advanced economies on average, despite higher volatility in economies that rely on commodity exports or are exposed to geopolitical tensions and political instability. Even if technological progress slows, as Gordon (2015) suggests, these countries will be able to use existing technologies to meet the growing needs of their expanding populations.

Previous studies have documented systematic statistical biases in forecasts. Ten- or 20-year forecasts have often been more optimistic than warranted, and the difference between actual and forecast growth is larger the longer the projection horizon (Ho and Mauro 2016). The analysis therefore examines an alternative (pessimistic) scenario alongside the baseline scenario. The alternative scenario can be viewed as measuring the economic costs of deviating from the policies needed to maintain strong growth consistent with the baseline forecasts. Such deviation often stems from geopolitical events or domestic political upheaval. Indeed, excessive optimism embedded in consensus projections of economic growth may largely reflect economic forecasters' reluctance to build low-probability, high-cost political events into their baseline economic projections.

The forecasting record is better for projections of population growth. Demographic developments are smoother than economic developments, and population growth is determined with long leads in the data. The forecasting record of the United Nations Population Division—one of the world's most widely respected forecasters of population—is good. Errors in population projections for the world as a whole have been limited (1–7 percent in various long-run projections), though errors in projections of population for individual countries have often been substantially larger. Across countries, the unweighted mean of the absolute errors observed ex post for individual country projections for the year 2000 made in 1980 was slightly greater than 10 percent (cumulative over the entire period), and the average bias was +2 percent (Bongaarts and Bulatao 2000). Errors were larger for smaller countries. They were also concentrated in projections of population growth among the very young and very old. The errors became smaller over time, presumably reflecting improvements in the quality of data inputs and forecasting techniques.

The estimates of global income inequality discussed in chapter 4 are robust to alternative population growth scenarios. The differences between the high- and low-fertility scenarios for 2035 are very small. The analysis throughout therefore draws only on the United Nations' medium-fertility scenario.

The population projections for individual countries and regions assume that international migration will be relatively low and in line with historical trends. In view of vast differences in demographic prospects across continents—including the demographic explosion in Africa, strong population growth in India, and population aging in most of the advanced economies—migration could well rise significantly. If it does, global inequality would likely narrow more rapidly than projected in the baseline scenario, because migrants would have higher incomes, their relatives at home would benefit from remittances, some migrants would return to their home countries with enhanced entrepreneurial know-how, and productive resources would arguably be allocated more efficiently.

Alternative Scenarios for Economic Growth Projections

Given concerns about the reliability of long-run economic growth forecasts—especially for countries that have grown rapidly over the past couple of decades, such as China and India (Pritchett and Summers 2014)—it makes sense to examine the effects of alternative assumptions.

Reversion to the Mean Scenario

The reversion to the mean scenario (based on projections by Ho and Mauro 2016) represents a more pessimistic outlook for convergence of the emerging-market economies' output levels toward those of the advanced economies, by assuming that each country's per capita growth gradually reverts to the global mean. It is based on a simple autoregressive process:

$$g_{2015-35} = \alpha + \beta g_{1994-2014}$$

where α and β are estimated through panel regressions applied to Penn World Tables data on real per capita GDP on 188 countries over 1950–2010 (subject to availability). Growth for the next two decades is projected by applying the estimated coefficients to a country's past growth (1994–2014). By allowing for some autocorrelation while projecting a gradual reversal toward the worldwide sample mean, this approach reduces the likelihood of overoptimistic projections stemming from excessive extrapolation of recent successes.

This alternative method has only a small effect on the projections for China, reducing its average growth rate over the next two decades from 4.2 to 4.0 percent, because the OECD projections in the baseline scenario already assume a gradual but significant slowing of Chinese growth after 2015. For India the difference between the baseline and the reversion to the mean scenario is larger (the average growth rates under the two scenarios are 4.7 and 2.6 percent).

The gap between the baseline and the reversion to the mean projections is larger, on average, for emerging-market economies than for advanced economies, reflecting the relatively weak performance of advanced economies during the past two decades (especially since the global economic and financial crisis that began in 2008). Consequently, the downward adjustment of projected income growth is larger for individuals lower down the global distribution of incomes. (Appendix table 2A.2 reports the baseline and alternative scenario projections for each economy in the sample.)

Given the high level of uncertainty about the economic prospects for Sub-Saharan Africa over the next two decades in the face of rapid population growth, the analysis also considers an even more pessimistic scenario, in which convergence of this region's economies halts and growth reverts to the global mean beginning in 2015.

Optimistic Scenario for the Most Populous Emerging-Market Economies

In an optimistic scenario, the emerging-market economies with the largest populations in 2035—India, China, Indonesia, and Nigeria—grow at significantly higher rates than in the baseline scenario. This scenario is included in order to determine the sensitivity of global developments to good economic policy and continued reform in these countries. It assumes that over the next 20 years, the annual GDP per capita growth rate for each of these large economies is higher than in the baseline by half the country's own historical standard deviation of growth; all other countries grow as in the baseline. Annual average per capita growth rates are thus 6.2 percent for China, 5.7 percent for India, 5.3 percent for Indonesia, and 6.0 percent for Nigeria. These growth rates are above the rates projected by Consensus Forecasts and significantly more optimistic than the OECD/IMF/World Bank forecasts used in the baseline scenario.[3]

---

3. Consensus Forecasts (www.consensuseconomics.com) polls more than 700 economists every month to obtain their forecasts and views.

Appendix 2A Sources of Data Used to Project Economic Growth

Most of the projections for economic growth come from existing sources. For many countries, including most of the largest economies, projections are available from more than one source. The differences across forecasters are relatively small. We generated our own projections for 62 smaller economies for which projections were not available from other sources.

GDP growth projections (for 2015–35) are from November 2015. They are drawn from the following sources (tables 2A.1 and 2A.2):

- Most of the data come from the OECD's Looking to 2060 website (www.oecd.org/eco/outlook/lookingto2060.htm). These projections are model-based and consistent with the projections published in the OECD's *Economic Outlook* (for a description of the methodology, see Johansson et al. 2013). The sources cover most advanced economies and a few large emerging-market economies.

- Where OECD projections were not available, projections from Consensus Forecasts were used. These projections are averages of several forecasts by various sources (such as Standard & Poor's, Credit Suisse, and Moody's Analytics), each using its own methodology. Consensus Forecasts are available only through 2024 or so. They were extended by assuming that growth in each subsequent year through 2035 was the same as in the last year for which projections were available. (The rationale for this approach is that most forecasters assume that the output gap is closed by the end of their projection period. The growth rate in the final projection year thus constitutes their best estimate of the country's potential growth rate.) This source allowed coverage to be extended to several emerging-market economies, especially in Eastern Europe, Asia, and Latin America.

- The OECD and Consensus Forecasts do not provide data on low-income countries (defined as countries eligible for assistance from the World Bank's International Development Association, which offers concessional loans and grants to the world's poorest countries). The main source of data for these countries is the most recent compilation of long-run economic growth projections in the debt sustainability analyses prepared by teams from the International Monetary Fund and World Bank.

- For countries for which projections are not available from any sources, we constructed them based on the following equation:

$$g_{2015-35} = \alpha + \beta g_{1994-2014}$$

where $\alpha = 2.0$ and $\beta = 0.25$. These coefficients were estimated through panel regressions applied to Penn World Tables data on real per capita GDP for 188 countries over 1950–2010, subject to availability (for details on the estimation, see Ho and Mauro 2016). Economic growth over the next two decades was projected on the basis of a simple autoregressive process (as in Pritchett and Summers 2014). In the case of the few countries for which data were not available over the past two decades or major wars dominated the 1990s/early 2000s, a similar autoregressive approach was used based on data for 2005–14.

Table 2A.1   Summary of sources of GDP growth projections

Source	Number of economies covered	Percent of 2015 world GDP (based on value in 2011 international dollars)
Organization for Economic Cooperation and Development (OECD)	40, including OECD members, Brazil, China, India, Indonesia, and Russia	79
Consensus Forecasts	16, including Hong Kong, Taiwan, Ukraine, and Venezuela	7
Teams from the International Monetary Fund and World Bank	69 low-income countries	4
$g_{2015-35} = \alpha + \beta g_{1994-2014}$	62 mostly low-income countries	10

Table 2A.2 Economic growth and population projections, by economy, 2015–35

Region/economy	Source	Average annual economic growth, 2015–35 (percent)			Percent of world GDP		Percent of world population	
		Per capita	Total	Reversion to the mean scenario	2014	2035	2014	2035
North America								
Canada	OECD	1.3	2.1	1.4	1.5	1.1	0.5	0.5
Mexico	OECD	2.1	3.1	1.2	2.0	1.8	1.8	1.8
United States	OECD	1.8	2.5	1.4	16.2	13.1	4.5	4.2
European Union								
Austria	OECD	1.8	2.0	1.4	0.4	0.3	0.1	0.1
Belgium	OECD	1.8	2.2	1.3	0.4	0.3	0.2	0.1
Bulgaria	Consensus Forecasts	3.0	2.1	2.0	0.1	0.1	0.1	0.1
Croatia	Consensus Forecasts	2.1	1.6	1.6	0.1	0.1	0.1	0.0
Cyprus	Authors	1.0	1.7	1.2	0.0	0.0	0.0	0.0
Czech Republic	OECD	3.2	3.0	1.7	0.3	0.3	0.1	0.1
Denmark	OECD	1.5	1.9	1.2	0.2	0.2	0.1	0.1
Estonia	OECD	3.2	2.8	2.5	0.0	0.0	0.0	0.0
Finland	OECD	2.0	2.2	1.6	0.2	0.2	0.1	0.1
France	OECD	2.0	2.3	1.2	2.3	1.8	0.9	0.8
Germany	OECD	1.2	1.1	1.3	3.4	2.0	1.1	0.9
Greece	OECD	3.4	3.1	1.1	0.3	0.2	0.2	0.1

(table continues)

17

Table 2A.2 Economic growth and population projections, by economy, 2015–35 *(continued)*

Region/economy	Source	Average annual economic growth, 2015–35 *(percent)*			Percent of world GDP		Percent of world population	
		Per capita	Total	Reversion to the mean scenario	2014	2035	2014	2035
European Union *(continued)*								
Hungary	OECD	2.3	1.9	1.6	0.2	0.2	0.1	0.1
Ireland	OECD	2.0	2.7	2.0	0.2	0.2	0.1	0.1
Italy	OECD	2.0	1.9	1.0	1.9	1.4	0.8	0.7
Latvia	Consensus Forecasts	2.9	2.3	2.6	0.0	0.0	0.0	0.0
Lithuania	Consensus Forecasts	3.4	2.8	2.4	0.1	0.1	0.0	0.0
Luxembourg	OECD	1.1	2.3	1.4	0.0	0.0	0.0	0.0
Malta	Authors	1.6	1.8	1.6	0.0	0.0	0.0	0.0
Netherlands	OECD	2.1	2.3	1.3	0.7	0.6	0.2	0.2
Poland	OECD	2.3	2.0	2.3	0.9	0.7	0.5	0.4
Portugal	OECD	2.4	2.1	1.2	0.3	0.2	0.1	0.1
Romania	Consensus Forecasts	3.4	2.7	2.0	0.4	0.3	0.3	0.2
Slovak Republic	OECD	2.7	2.5	2.2	0.1	0.1	0.1	0.1
Slovenia	OECD	2.3	2.2	1.7	0.1	0.0	0.0	0.0
Spain	OECD	2.0	1.9	1.3	1.5	1.0	0.6	0.5
Sweden	OECD	1.9	2.5	1.6	0.4	0.3	0.1	0.1
United Kingdom	OECD	2.1	2.6	1.5	2.4	2.0	0.9	0.8

Other OECD

Australia	OECD	2.1	3.2	1.5	1.0	0.9	0.3	0.3
Chile	OECD	3.3	4.1	2.0	0.4	0.4	0.2	0.2
Iceland	OECD	1.5	2.1	1.5	0.0	0.0	0.0	0.0
Israel	OECD	1.6	3.1	1.5	0.2	0.2	0.1	0.1
Japan	OECD	1.5	1.1	1.1	4.4	2.7	1.8	1.4
Korea	OECD	2.5	2.7	2.3	1.6	1.4	0.7	0.6
New Zealand	OECD	1.8	2.5	1.5	0.1	0.1	0.1	0.1
Norway	OECD	1.4	2.3	1.4	0.3	0.2	0.1	0.1
Switzerland	OECD	1.4	2.1	1.2	0.4	0.3	0.1	0.1
Turkey	OECD	3.4	4.2	1.7	1.4	1.6	1.1	1.0

China

China	OECD	4.2	4.4	4.0	16.8	20.3	19.2	16.3
Hong Kong	Consensus Forecasts	2.7	3.3	1.7	0.4	0.3	0.1	0.1
Macao	Authors	3.2	4.5	2.9	0.1	0.1	0.0	0.0
India	OECD	4.7	5.7	2.6	6.9	10.7	18.2	18.3

(table continues)

Table 2A.2 Economic growth and population projections, by economy, 2015–35 (continued)

Region/economy	Source	Average annual economic growth, 2015–35 (percent)			Percent of world GDP		Percent of world population	
		Per capita	Total	Reversion to the mean scenario	2014	2035	2014	2035
Latin America and the Caribbean								
Antigua and Barbuda	Authors	1.0	1.9	1.1	0.0	0.0	0.0	0.0
Argentina	Consensus Forecasts	2.7	3.6	—	0.8	0.8	0.6	0.6
Bahamas, The	Authors	1.1	2.0	1.0	0.0	0.0	0.0	0.0
Barbados	Authors	2.1	2.2	1.3	0.0	0.0	0.0	0.0
Belize	Authors	1.3	3.0	1.3	0.0	0.0	0.0	0.0
Bermuda	Authors	1.3	1.0	1.3	0.0	0.0	0.0	0.0
Bolivia	IMF/World Bank	2.6	3.9	1.6	0.1	0.1	0.1	0.2
Brazil	OECD	2.0	2.6	1.5	3.0	2.5	2.9	2.7
Colombia	Consensus Forecasts	3.6	4.3	1.5	0.6	0.7	0.7	0.6
Costa Rica	Authors	1.5	2.3	1.7	0.1	0.1	0.1	0.1
Dominica	IMF/World Bank	1.3	1.6	1.4	0.0	0.0	0.0	0.0
Dominican Republic	Authors	1.7	2.6	2.1	0.1	0.1	0.1	0.1
Ecuador	Authors	1.1	2.4	1.4	0.2	0.1	0.2	0.2
El Salvador	Authors	1.3	1.6	1.5	0.0	0.0	0.1	0.1
Grenada	IMF/World Bank	2.5	2.8	1.6	0.0	0.0	0.0	0.0
Guatemala	Authors	1.3	3.1	1.2	0.1	0.1	0.2	0.3

Latin America and the Caribbean

Guyana	IMF/World Bank	2.9	3.2	1.6	0.0	0.0	0.0
Haiti	IMF/World Bank	3.7	4.8	1.3	0.0	0.1	0.2
Honduras	IMF/World Bank	1.5	2.7	1.3	0.0	0.1	0.1
Jamaica	Authors	0.9	1.0	0.9	0.0	0.0	0.0
Nicaragua	IMF/World Bank	2.7	3.7	1.6	0.0	0.1	0.1
Panama	Authors	2.0	3.3	2.2	0.1	0.1	0.1
Paraguay	Authors	0.9	2.0	1.3	0.0	0.1	0.1
Peru	Consensus Forecasts	4.4	5.4	2.2	0.5	0.4	0.4
Puerto Rico	Authors	1.2	1.1	1.2	0.1	0.1	0.0
St. Kitts and Nevis	Authors	1.1	1.9	1.3	0.0	0.0	0.0
St. Lucia	IMF/World Bank	2.2	2.8	1.2	0.0	0.0	0.0
St. Vincent and the Grenadines	IMF/World Bank	3.2	3.3	1.7	0.0	0.0	0.0
Suriname	Authors	1.7	2.4	1.7	0.0	0.0	0.0
Uruguay	Authors	1.7	2.0	1.8	0.1	0.0	0.0
Venezuela	Consensus Forecasts	1.9	3.0	1.0	0.5	0.4	0.4

(table continues)

Table 2A.2 Economic growth and population projections, by economy, 2015–35 *(continued)*

Region/economy	Source	Average annual economic growth, 2015–35 (percent)			Percent of world GDP		Percent of world population	
		Per capita	Total	Reversion to the mean scenario	2014	2035	2014	2035
East Asia and the Pacific								
Brunei Darussalam	Authors	0.4	1.4	0.7	0.0	0.0	0.0	0.0
Cambodia	IMF/World Bank	6.1	7.5	2.7	0.0	0.1	0.2	0.2
Fiji	Authors	1.3	1.6	1.2	0.0	0.0	0.0	0.0
Indonesia	OECD	4.3	5.2	1.9	2.5	3.5	3.6	3.5
Kiribati	IMF/World Bank	0.7	2.2	1.3	0.0	0.0	0.0	0.0
Lao People's Democratic Republic	IMF/World Bank	4.9	6.4	2.6	0.0	0.1	0.1	0.1
Malaysia	Consensus Forecasts	4.7	5.8	1.9	0.7	1.1	0.4	0.4
Marshall Islands	Authors	1.1	1.6	1.1	0.0	0.0	0.0	0.0
Micronesia	Authors	1.2	1.9	1.0	0.0	0.0	0.0	0.0
Mongolia	IMF/World Bank	4.4	5.5	2.6	0.0	0.0	0.0	0.0
Palau	Authors	1.3	2.3	1.1	0.0	0.0	0.0	0.0
Papua New Guinea	IMF/World Bank	2.3	4.2	1.0	0.0	0.0	0.1	0.1
Philippines	Consensus Forecasts	5.2	6.6	1.7	0.6	1.2	1.4	1.5
Samoa	IMF/World Bank	1.3	2.0	1.6	0.0	0.0	0.0	0.0
Singapore	Consensus Forecasts	2.9	3.7	2.0	0.4	0.4	0.1	0.1
Solomon Islands	IMF/World Bank	1.4	3.1	0.8	0.0	0.0	0.0	0.0

East Asia and the Pacific

Taiwan	Consensus Forecasts	2.3	2.2	—	1.0	0.7	0.3	0.3
Thailand	Consensus Forecasts	3.3	3.3	1.8	0.9	0.9	1.0	0.8
Timor-Leste	IMF/World Bank	2.9	4.8	2.9	0.0	0.0	0.0	0.0
Tonga	IMF/World Bank	1.2	2.0	1.3	0.0	0.0	0.0	0.0
Tuvalu	Authors	1.3	1.8	1.4	0.0	0.0	0.0	0.0
Vanuatu	IMF/World Bank	1.9	3.9	1.1	0.0	0.0	0.0	0.0
Vietnam	IMF/World Bank	6.7	7.5	2.7	0.5	1.1	1.3	1.2
South Asia								
Afghanistan	IMF/World Bank	2.7	4.7	—	0.1	0.1	0.4	0.5
Bangladesh	IMF/World Bank	4.7	5.7	2.2	0.5	0.7	2.2	2.2
Bhutan	IMF/World Bank	5.1	6.0	2.7	0.0	0.0	0.0	0.0
Maldives	IMF/World Bank	1.9	3.1	2.4	0.0	0.0	0.0	0.0
Nepal	IMF/World Bank	3.0	3.9	1.7	0.1	0.1	0.4	0.4
Pakistan	Authors	1.5	3.2	1.5	0.8	0.8	2.6	3.0
Sri Lanka	Authors	2.3	2.5	2.4	0.2	0.2	0.3	0.2

(table continues)

Table 2A.2 Economic growth and population projections, by economy, 2015–35 *(continued)*

Region/economy	Source	Average annual economic growth, 2015–35 (percent)			Percent of world GDP		Percent of world population	
		Per capita	Total	Reversion to the mean scenario	2014	2035	2014	2035
Middle East and North Africa								
Algeria	Authors	1.3	2.5	1.4	0.5	0.4	0.5	0.6
Bahrain	Authors	0.7	1.8	0.8	0.1	0.0	0.0	0.0
Djibouti	IMF/World Bank	4.7	5.8	1.1	0.0	0.0	0.0	0.0
Egypt	Authors	2.2	3.9	1.8	0.9	0.9	1.3	1.5
Iran	Authors	1.5	2.2	1.6	1.2	0.9	1.1	1.0
Iraq	Authors	4.0	6.8	3.6	0.5	0.9	0.5	0.7
Jordan	Authors	1.7	3.0	1.6	0.1	0.1	0.1	0.1
Lebanon	Authors	1.6	1.4	1.5	0.1	0.1	0.1	0.1
Libya	Authors	2.5	3.5	0.9	0.1	0.1	0.1	0.1
Morocco	Authors	1.9	2.9	1.8	0.2	0.2	0.5	0.5
Oman	Authors	1.5	2.6	1.4	0.2	0.1	0.1	0.1
Qatar	Authors	1.2	2.6	1.6	0.3	0.2	0.0	0.0
Saudi Arabia	Authors	1.8	3.2	1.5	1.5	1.4	0.4	0.5
Tunisia	Authors	1.9	2.7	1.9	0.1	0.1	0.2	0.1
United Arab Emirates	Authors	-0.7	0.4	-0.2	0.6	0.3	0.1	0.1
West Bank and Gaza	Authors	1.8	1.8	1.8	0.0	0.0	0.0	0.0
Yemen	IMF/World Bank	2.9	4.9	1.0	0.1	0.1	0.4	0.5

Sub-Saharan Africa

Angola	Authors	3.0	6.1	2.6	0.2	0.3	0.3	0.5
Benin	IMF/World Bank	2.5	4.9	1.2	0.0	0.0	0.1	0.2
Botswana	Authors	1.9	3.4	1.9	0.0	0.0	0.0	0.0
Burkina Faso	IMF/World Bank	3.8	6.6	1.9	0.0	0.1	0.2	0.4
Burundi	IMF/World Bank	3.4	6.4	0.4	0.0	0.0	0.2	0.2
Cabo Verde	IMF/World Bank	4.9	6.0	3.0	0.0	0.0	0.0	0.0
Cameroon	IMF/World Bank	2.2	4.5	1.2	0.1	0.1	0.3	0.4
Central African Republic	IMF/World Bank	4.7	6.7	0.6	0.0	0.0	0.1	0.1
Chad	IMF/World Bank	1.1	4.1	2.1	0.0	0.0	0.2	0.3
Comoros	IMF/World Bank	2.7	4.8	0.6	0.0	0.0	0.0	0.0
Congo, Democratic Republic of	IMF/World Bank	2.1	5.0	0.7	0.1	0.1	1.1	1.6
Congo, Republic of	IMF/World Bank	1.6	4.2	1.0	0.0	0.0	0.1	0.1
Côte d'Ivoire	IMF/World Bank	3.4	5.8	0.9	0.1	0.1	0.3	0.4
Equatorial Guinea	Authors	7.2	9.9	6.3	0.0	0.1	0.0	0.0

(table continues)

Table 2A.2 Economic growth and population projections, by economy, 2015–35 *(continued)*

| Region/economy | Source | Average annual economic growth, 2015–35 (percent) | | | Percent of world GDP | | Percent of world population | |
		Per capita	Total	Reversion to the mean scenario	2014	2035	2014	2035
Sub-Saharan Africa *(continued)*								
Eritrea	IMF/World Bank	–0.9	1.3	0.8	0.0	0.0	0.1	0.1
Ethiopia	IMF/World Bank	4.2	6.4	2.3	0.1	0.2	1.4	1.8
Gabon	Authors	1.0	3.0	0.8	0.0	0.0	0.0	0.0
Gambia	IMF/World Bank	3.3	6.4	1.0	0.0	0.0	0.0	0.0
Ghana	IMF/World Bank	3.7	5.8	2.0	0.1	0.2	0.4	0.5
Guinea	IMF/World Bank	4.2	6.7	1.1	0.0	0.0	0.2	0.2
Guinea-Bissau	IMF/World Bank	2.0	4.1	0.4	0.0	0.0	0.0	0.0
Kenya	IMF/World Bank	2.6	5.0	1.1	0.1	0.2	0.6	0.8
Lesotho	IMF/World Bank	4.3	5.4	1.8	0.0	0.0	0.0	0.0
Liberia	IMF/World Bank	3.9	6.4	3.4	0.0	0.0	0.1	0.1
Madagascar	IMF/World Bank	3.9	6.6	0.7	0.0	0.1	0.3	0.5
Malawi	IMF/World Bank	3.0	6.0	1.3	0.0	0.0	0.2	0.4
Mali	IMF/World Bank	2.1	5.1	1.5	0.0	0.0	0.2	0.4
Mauritania	IMF/World Bank	1.4	3.6	1.3	0.0	0.0	0.1	0.1
Mauritius	Authors	1.8	1.9	2.0	0.0	0.0	0.0	0.0
Mozambique	IMF/World Bank	5.9	8.7	2.3	0.0	0.1	0.4	0.5
Namibia	Authors	1.8	3.7	1.6	0.0	0.0	0.0	0.0

Sub-Saharan Africa

Niger	IMF/World Bank	2.2	6.3	1.0	0.0	0.0	0.3	0.5
Nigeria	IMF/World Bank	4.3	6.8	2.0	1.0	1.9	2.5	3.4
Rwanda	IMF/World Bank	3.7	5.8	1.5	0.0	0.0	0.2	0.2
São Tomé and Príncipe	IMF/World Bank	4.0	6.0	2.0	0.0	0.0	0.0	0.0
Senegal	IMF/World Bank	2.8	5.6	1.2	0.0	0.0	0.2	0.3
Seychelles	Authors	1.3	1.5	1.5	0.0	0.0	0.0	0.0
Sierra Leone	IMF/World Bank	4.0	5.9	1.7	0.0	0.0	0.1	0.1
South Africa	OECD	4.0	4.6	1.3	0.7	0.8	0.8	0.7
Sudan	IMF/World Bank	1.5	3.7	1.7	0.1	0.2	0.6	0.7
Swaziland	Authors	1.5	2.6	1.2	0.0	0.0	0.0	0.0
Tanzania	IMF/World Bank	2.9	5.9	1.8	0.1	0.2	0.7	1.1
Togo	IMF/World Bank	1.9	4.4	1.3	0.0	0.0	0.1	0.1
Trinidad and Tobago	Authors	2.3	2.4	2.3	0.0	0.0	0.0	0.0
Uganda	IMF/World Bank	2.9	6.1	2.0	0.1	0.1	0.5	0.8
Zambia	IMF/World Bank	3.0	6.0	1.2	0.1	0.1	0.2	0.3
Zimbabwe	IMF/World Bank	1.1	3.2	0.3	0.0	0.0	0.2	0.3

(table continues)

Table 2A.2 Economic growth and population projections, by economy, 2015–35 (continued)

Region/economy	Source	Average annual economic growth, 2015–35 (percent)			Percent of world GDP		Percent of world population	
		Per capita	Total	Reversion to the mean scenario	2014	2035	2014	2035
Eastern Europe and Central Asia								
Albania	Authors	3.3	3.3	2.9	0.0	0.0	0.0	0.0
Armenia	IMF/World Bank	4.4	4.3	3.3	0.0	0.0	0.0	0.0
Azerbaijan	Authors	3.1	3.7	3.0	0.2	0.2	0.1	0.1
Belarus	Authors	2.5	2.1	2.5	0.2	0.1	0.1	0.1
Bosnia and Herzegovina	Authors	2.1	1.6	2.2	0.0	0.0	0.1	0.0
Georgia	IMF/World Bank	5.7	5.3	2.7	0.0	0.0	0.1	0.0
Kazakhstan	Authors	2.3	3.1	2.3	0.4	0.4	0.2	0.2
Kyrgyz Republic	IMF/World Bank	3.9	5.1	1.4	0.0	0.0	0.1	0.1
Macedonia	Authors	1.3	1.3	1.5	0.0	0.0	0.0	0.0
Moldova	IMF/World Bank	5.8	5.4	1.2	0.0	0.0	0.1	0.0
Montenegro	Authors	2.4	2.2	2.3	0.0	0.0	0.0	0.0
Russia	OECD	3.0	2.8	1.7	3.3	2.8	2.0	1.6
Serbia	Authors	1.8	1.4	2.0	0.1	0.1	0.1	0.1
Tajikistan	IMF/World Bank	3.0	4.8	1.3	0.0	0.0	0.1	0.1
Turkmenistan	Authors	1.9	2.7	2.2	0.1	0.1	0.1	0.1
Ukraine	Consensus Forecasts	2.8	2.1	1.1	0.4	0.3	0.6	0.5
Uzbekistan	Authors	1.9	2.8	2.1	0.2	0.1	0.4	0.4

— = not available

3

Measuring Income Distribution within Countries

The test of our progress is not whether we add more to the abundance of those who have much; it is whether we provide enough for those who have too little.

—Franklin D. Roosevelt

In many countries, large and growing domestic income disparities have pushed their way to the top of the list of citizens' concerns. To many people, the growing gap between the haves and the have-nots indicates a failure of the political and economic system to treat all citizens with equal concern and respect. The moral issue is reason enough to pay close attention to how inequality is measured, how it compares across countries, and how it evolves over time.

There is also a practical reason to focus on the measurement of inequality. Unpacking the detail hiding behind macroeconomic measures of national well-being—focusing on people rather than countries—requires information on how living standards are distributed among a country's citizens. Measuring inequality within countries is crucial for estimating global inequality. Moreover, estimates of domestic distributions and judgments about how they are likely to evolve in the future will influence the projected evolution of the gap between the global rich and the global poor, as well as the global consumption of various categories of goods and services.

This chapter examines how economists measure inequality. It discusses the challenges posed by survey data and explains a novel method of reconciling surveys with national account measures of household consumption. This method results in higher estimates of inequality within countries than indicated by survey data alone. The chapter then discusses recent trends in inequality within countries and the cross-country relationship between inequality and the level of development. The results can be used to inform projections of within-country inequality into the future.

How Do Economists Measure Inequality? Key Concepts and Issues

The most straightforward way of finding out about individuals' incomes or consumption is to ask them directly. A household survey can provide a good approximation of the distribution of living standards in the population at large, provided that its sample is nationally representative and respondents answer honestly.

The Gini Index

Suppose all households participating in a survey are lined up in ascending order of household income. How would one capture the income disparities between them in a single number? Many measures have been put forward over the years, with different properties and varying degrees of relevance, depending on the specific question one is trying to answer (see Cowell 2011 for a discussion).

The best-known and most widely used measure of inequality is the Gini index (also referred to as the Gini coefficient). It is presented by means of the Lorenz curve, which plots the proportion of the total income of the population that is cumulatively earned by the bottom x percent of the population. The Gini index is equal to the ratio of the area (G) between the Lorenz curve and the line of perfect equality to the area of the triangle ABC in figure 3.1. It takes values between 0 and 100. Perfect equality is achieved when the bottom x percent of the population receives x percent of total income, in which case the Lorenz curve overlaps with the line of perfect equality and the Gini index equals zero. Perfect inequality occurs when all income goes to a single person, in which case the Lorenz curve is ABC in figure 3.1 and the Gini index equals 100.

Use of Income or Consumption

In an ideal world, all countries would survey households on a consistent basis, using identical concepts and methodologies, so that survey results would be directly comparable across countries. In the real world, household surveys are not designed by national statistical agencies with international comparability in mind.

The analysis here uses the best survey data available, primarily from the Luxembourg Income Study (LIS), which collects income survey data on a large number of middle- and high-income countries; harmonizes them to enable cross-national comparisons; and makes them available for public use. Information on countries not covered by the LIS is obtained from the World Bank database, which is based largely on consumption surveys. This

Figure 3.1 The Lorenz curve and the Gini index

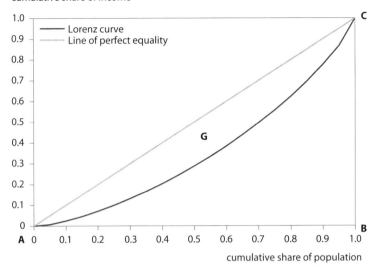

cumulative share of income

Source: Authors' illustration.

mixing of income and consumption surveys is far from ideal, but given data constraints it has become the standard approach in the literature.[1]

There are good practical reasons why some countries survey household incomes and others survey consumption. As Angus Deaton (2005, 5) notes, "consumption is typically much easier to measure in surveys than is income in poor countries, where many people are self-employed in agriculture, whereas the opposite is true in rich countries, where most people are wage earners and are more reluctant to cooperate with time-consuming consumption surveys." Combining income and consumption data, although questionable in principle, can therefore potentially increase the accuracy of cross-country comparisons of inequality and estimates of the global distribution of individual living standards. (For a description of the sources of the household survey data used in this chapter, see appendix 3A.)

---

1. Within countries consumption tends to be more equally distributed than income, because household saving rates generally increase with income, richer households have better access to credit and can thus borrow to maintain their consumption when their incomes fall temporarily, and low-income rural households in emerging-market economies sustain their consumption by producing goods and services at home.

Correcting for Underreporting of Incomes and Undersampling of Rich Households

Survey data suffer from measurement errors that can significantly affect estimates of domestic and global inequality. In particular, respondents do not always honestly report certain components of income. For example, income from self-employment is often underreported, because self-employed respondents who have understated their tax liability in tax returns may fear self-incrimination if they report their income accurately in household surveys.

Surveys are also not always representative of the population. In particular, they often suffer from undersampling of high-income households, which tend to have lower response rates (perhaps because the opportunity cost of the time spent filling out a questionnaire rises with income).

These sources of error likely help explain the gap between the total income or consumption recorded in surveys and the often larger measures of household income or consumption in national accounts (Anand and Segal 2008). Many researchers have noted this gap, but consensus on its sources and the appropriate method to deal with it has proved elusive (Bhalla 2002; Cline 2004; Deaton 2005; Milanović 2005; Anand and Segal 2008, 2015; Chen and Ravallion 2010; Pinkovskiy and Sala-i-Martín 2010; Lakner and Milanović 2016).

This chapter uses a novel approach to adjust the survey data for these sources of error and to reconcile them with data on household final consumption expenditure in the national accounts. The approach involves two adjustments. First, the incomes of the self-employed are increased, more so in countries with large shares of self-employment in total employment and countries with lower institutional quality, where tax evasion is likely to be more widespread.

Second, the number of people in the upper tail of the distribution is increased (and the number in the rest of the distribution decreased, in order to maintain an unchanged population) to correct for the fact that high-income households often refuse to participate in surveys and tend to underreport their incomes when they do.[2] This adjustment consists of splicing a thicker upper tail onto the survey distribution in a way that maintains a smooth and continuous bell-shaped curve. The adjusted upper tail follows the Pareto distribution, which Wilfredo Pareto (1848–1923)

2. Some researchers have attempted to correct for undersampling of high-income households in surveys by using administrative records (such as tax returns) to design more representative samples. A good example is the Federal Reserve Board's Survey of Consumer Finances in the United States (Bricker et al. 2015). Such data are not available for the vast majority of countries, precluding use of this approach here.

showed is a good approximation of the distribution of income among rich households.[3] Anthony B. Atkinson, Thomas Piketty, and Emmanuel Saez (2007, 2010) corroborated his findings using the tax records of the richest taxpayers in many advanced and emerging-market economies. These adjustments eliminate the gap between income/consumption reported in surveys and the estimate of household final consumption expenditure in the national accounts. (For details on the adjustment method and the justification for it, see appendix 3B.)

The adjustments significantly affect estimates of domestic inequality. Figure 3.2 compares the Gini index obtained using only the raw survey data in the LIS sample of countries with the Gini index obtained after adjusting for the underreporting of self-employment income and the undersampling of rich households. The adjustment increases inequality significantly in all countries, primarily because of the adjustment of the upper tail. The effect is largest in countries where the gap was initially large and self-employment low, so that the adjustment to the upper tail is relatively large. This group includes many emerging-market economies as well as the United States and several countries in Central, Eastern, and Southern Europe.

Recent Trends in Within-Country Inequality

This book is about the future. But in order to make informed forecasts about what lies ahead, it can be useful to briefly look at what happened in the recent past.

Some advanced economies, particularly the United States and the United Kingdom, have seen growing public concern about rising inequality over the past three decades. This trend is visible in survey data; it is particularly stark in data from tax returns, which are better than surveys at capturing the incomes of the richest households. Studies based on tax return data (notably, Atkinson, Piketty, and Saez 2011) show that the shares of income accruing to the top percentiles of the population in the United States and a few other (mostly advanced) have been growing since the 1980s. Viewed

---

3. The probability density function of the Pareto distribution, describing the relative likelihood that a random variable x takes on a given value, is given by the following equation:

$$f_X(x) = \begin{cases} 1 - \left(\frac{x_m}{x}\right)^\alpha & \text{if } x \geq x_m \\ 0 & \text{if } x < x_m \end{cases}$$

The probability density function of the Pareto distribution takes positive values only above a certain minimum, x_m. Its slope is initially steep and flattens gradually as x increases; eventually, it converges to zero. The Pareto distribution is characterized by two parameters: a scale parameter, x_m, and a shape parameter α, also known as the tail index. The latter indicates the thickness of the upper tail—the speed with which it converges to zero. Lower values of α indicate a thicker tail (slower convergence to zero) and more income inequality.

Figure 3.2   Within-country inequality before and after adjusting for underreporting of incomes and undersampling of rich households

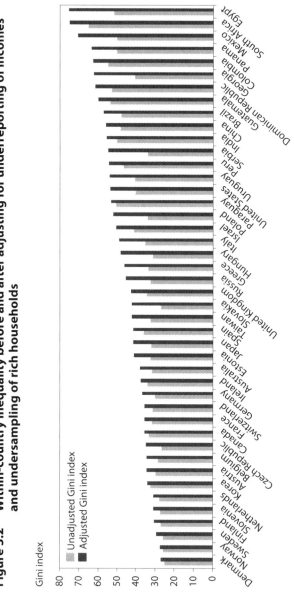

Gini index

Unadjusted Gini index
Adjusted Gini index

Note: The figure is based on the most recent data available for each country. Data for Austria, China, Guatemala, Korea, Sweden, and Switzerland are from the early to mid-2000s. All other data are from the late 2000s or early 2010s (see appendix table 3A.1).

Sources: Luxembourg Income Study for disposable income; World Bank national accounts data for household final consumption expenditure.

from London or New York it may seem that, absent significant changes in policy, within-country inequality is destined to continue increasing, as the people with the greatest talent or the luckiest start in life seem set to capture an increasing share of the economic pie.

It would be misleading, however, to base expectations about developments in within-country inequality across the globe on the recent experience of a few economies. Data from tax returns show that the rich are not increasing their share of total income in all advanced economies. Inequality has remained stable or decreased in several advanced economies (including Australia, Finland, New Zealand, Norway, and Spain) over the past 15 years, according to the World Wealth and Income Database (www.wid.world).

To obtain a more complete picture of within-country inequality across the globe, it is necessary to cast a wider net, considering a broader range of countries and studying the full income distribution rather than just the incomes of people at the top. Doing so requires analyzing household survey data in addition to tax returns. Survey data from the LIS and the World Bank's database show that since 1995 (99 countries) and 2000 (114 countries), half of the countries in the sample experienced a reduction in the Gini index (reduced inequality) of more than one point (on a 0–100 scale), a third experienced an increase (increased inequality) of more than one point, and the remainder experienced changes of less than one point (in either direction).

Because household surveys tend to underrepresent the richest households, they may fail to fully capture the rising share of income going to the very top. When survey data are adjusted for underreporting of self-employment income and undersampling of rich households, recent trends in inequality remain mixed. Out of 102 countries with at least two data points after 2000 that are more than five years apart, 47 saw a reduction in inequality of more than one Gini point in that interval, 39 experienced an increase of more than one point, and the remaining 16 experienced changes of less than one point (in either direction).

Relationship between Inequality and Development

When thinking about future developments in a growing world economy, it is important to consider the possibility that distributional patterns in advanced economies on the one hand and emerging-market economies on the other will differ. Social and economic changes are more rapid and disruptive in the latter group, which may be reflected in the distribution of living standards there.

Historically, a multitude of factors has affected the distribution of income (or consumption) within countries. These factors vary across countries and over time. Studies seeking to unveil potential determinants of changes in within-country inequality have focused on changes in GDP, using two approaches.

The first, simpler, approach examines whether growth is good for the poor. It analyzes the empirical association between growth in real per capita GDP and the share of GDP accruing to the bottom of the distribution. This research finds no significant evidence of systematic effects of economic growth on the distribution of incomes. In their study of 118 countries over the past four decades, David Dollar, Tatjana Kleineberg, and Aart Kraay (2013) find that changes in the share of income accruing to the bottom two quintiles in individual countries are generally small and uncorrelated with changes in average income. In a similar panel of countries, they find that changes in overall income are the primary driver of changes in social welfare (measured by various measures of overall income and inequality); changes in inequality play a relatively minor role (Dollar, Kleineberg, and Kraay 2014).[4]

The second approach tests Simon Kuznets' (1955) hypothesis, according to which inequality first increases as a country grows wealthier before decreasing (the Kuznets curve). According to Kuznets, in the early stages of economic development, economic growth occurs by shifting workers from lower-productivity agriculture to higher-productivity industry. Inequality initially increases, as incomes rise for capitalists and urban workers while wages remain stable in the countryside, where labor remains abundant and productivity low. Eventually, as industrialization and urbanization become widespread and the middle class achieves critical mass, the modern welfare state expands and inequality starts to fall. Shrinking rural populations lead to the substitution of capital for labor in agriculture, boosting productivity and reducing wage differentials between urban and rural workers.

The Kuznets hypothesis is intuitively appealing for emerging-market economies that are undergoing the structural transformation from agriculture to industry before maturing to a more modern mix of agriculture, industry, and services. It is less applicable to mature advanced economies during the past two or three decades.

The Kuznets curve–based approach has generated a vast number of empirical studies. Many are inconclusive (Ravallion and Chen 1997,

---

4. Even so, convergence in the mean incomes of developing countries is not accompanied by convergence in poverty rates, and high initial poverty is associated with lower subsequent economic growth and a weaker impact of such growth on poverty (Ravallion 2012).

Deininger and Squire 1998) or find limited supportive evidence (Barro 2000; Higgins and Williamson 2002; Bhandari, Pradhan, and Upadhyay 2010). The evidence has been stronger for cross sections of countries (international comparisons of countries at one point in time) than for time series (changes over time within individual countries) (Desbordes and Verardi 2012).

A potential explanation for the lack of conclusive evidence in favor of the Kuznets hypothesis is that the distributional data based on household surveys suffer from measurement error and lack of international comparability. Some of the sources of error (discussed in appendix 3B), especially the undersampling of relatively rich households, are likely to be more severe in middle-income countries than in either poor countries or advanced economies, because richer households in these countries often live in gated communities, out of reach of survey fieldwork officers. Larger measurement error for middle-income countries would tend to weaken the observed statistical associations between per capita GDP and within-country inequality.

When the survey data are adjusted for underreporting by the self-employed and undersampling of the richest households, the Kuznets hypothesis finds considerable support in a large cross section of countries. Figure 3.3 plots the Gini index against per capita final household consumption expenditure in the national accounts for the 110 countries for which survey data were adjusted. A quadratic (unweighted) regression of the Gini index on household final consumption expenditure per capita explains a third of the variation in the Gini indices across countries. By comparison, the share explained in the unadjusted data for the same sample of countries is only 8 percent.

Driving the improvement in the fit of the Kuznets curve is the adjustment to the upper tail of the distribution. The gap between survey means and household consumption per capita in the national accounts is largest in lower-middle- and middle-income countries, where the underreporting of income and the undersampling of rich households is likely to be greatest.

Projections of Within-Country Inequality

The analysis in the coming chapters requires judgment about the most likely path of within-country inequality over the next 20 years. Two scenarios are examined. The baseline assumes no change in within-country inequality. An alternative scenario assumes that within-country inequality follows the path indicated by the best-fit line in figure 3.3.

Figure 3.3   Evidence of the Kuznets curve based on data from 110 countries

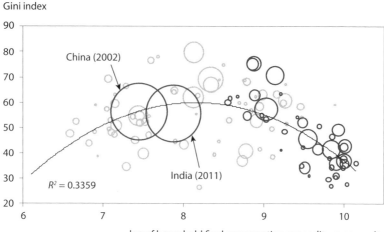

Gini index

log of household final consumption expenditure per capita
(in purchasing power parity dollars)

Note: The figure is based on the most recent data available for each country. The size of the bubbles is proportional to each country's population. Countries in the Luxembourg Income Study sample are marked in dark gray. The United States is excluded because it is an outlier and because the Kuznets relationship would not be expected to hold in the richest countries in the world.

Sources: Luxembourg Income Study and World Bank PovcalNet database for within-country Gini indices; World Bank national accounts data for household final consumption expenditure.

Projections Assuming Inequality Remains at Current Levels

The baseline projections assume that inequality within countries will remain at its estimated 2015 level. In this scenario all individual incomes grow in line with per capita GDP in each country; the distribution of income within countries thus remains unchanged.[5]

Constant within-country inequality over the next 20 years is a simplifying working assumption. As recent trends illustrate, there is no reason to believe that inequality will remain unchanged in all countries of the world. Inequality is likely to rise in some countries and fall in others. The factors that affect inequality are multiple and complex. It is therefore difficult to

---

5. An exception is made for China, where consumption rather than income data are used, and the household saving rate, which is extremely high by international standards, is assumed to revert to its 2000 level by 2035. As a result, household consumption per capita in China is projected to grow at an average annual rate of 5.5 percent (compared with 4.2 percent for per capita GDP). Inequality in China is assumed to remain unchanged.

form a judgment about their likely path 20 years into the future and to predict within-country inequality with any degree of confidence.

One might be tempted instead to extrapolate recent trends on a country-by-country basis. Doing so would be inappropriate, for two reasons. First, the data on inequality in some countries are not always calculated on a consistent basis over time, making the estimation of trends problematic, and several countries have insufficient data to calculate a trend accurately. Second, even for countries with good data, the trend has not been steady over the past few decades. Many countries saw a significant increase in inequality in the 1980s and 1990s and a more limited rise or even decline in the 2000s. The choice of timeframe over which the trend is calculated is therefore significant. Judgments about the causes of past changes and their continued relevance are difficult to make.

Projections Based on the Kuznets Hypothesis

One factor that appears to have significant influence on within-country inequality in a cross-country context is the level of development. Economic growth is something for which informed projections exist (chapter 2). It is therefore possible to consider an alternative scenario in which within-country inequality is projected to follow the path traced by the best-fitting line in figure 3.3.

The quadratic relationship between the Gini index and the household final consumption expenditure shown in figure 3.3 is used to project the change in the Gini index for each country. Each country's dot is moved horizontally in line with projected growth rates and vertically so as to maintain a constant distance between it and the line of best fit. This process results in rising inequality in the poorest countries that are on the upward sloping part of the curve and falling inequality in countries near or past the peak of the curve (logarithm of consumption equal to 8.16, or consumption of $3,502 a year). This latter group includes the most populous countries in Asia.

This scenario imposes a restriction that the within-country Gini index for middle-income countries moving along the downward part of the Kuznets curve cannot fall below 45, corresponding roughly to the 75th percentile of the distribution of Gini indices in advanced countries. The relationship in figure 3.3 is assumed to hold only for countries with logarithm per capita household consumption below 9.5 ($13,360 a year), in line with the observation that the Kuznets hypothesis is not relevant for advanced economies. For countries above this threshold, inequality is assumed to remain unchanged, as in the baseline scenario.

Figure 3.4 shows the countries with the largest projected changes in the within-country Gini index between 2015 and 2035. Countries starting off

Figure 3.4 Countries with the largest projected changes in within-country inequality between 2015 and 2035 under the alternative ("Kuznets") scenario

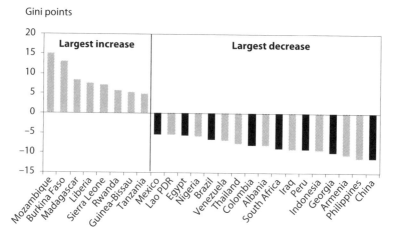

Note: The projected changes are expressed relative to the 2015 estimates of adjusted Gini indices. Countries in the Luxembourg Income Study sample are marked in black.

Sources: Luxembourg Income Study and World Bank PovcalNet database for data on within-country Gini indices; World Bank national accounts data for household final consumption expenditure.

poor but projected to grow rapidly are expected to see the largest increase in inequality; the fast-growing countries on the downward sloping part of the Kuznets curve are expected to see the largest declines in inequality.

This scenario is considered as an alternative rather than the baseline, because evidence on the Kuznets relationship within countries over time is less conclusive than evidence across countries. More work needs to be done on the adjusted data in a time-series setting before assessing how informative this relationship is for projecting inequality within countries over the next 20 years.

Some researchers (notably Milanović 2016) have begun to think about structural factors that might lead the Kuznets curve to slope upward again at high levels of development, in line with the recent experience of leading advanced economies, such as the United States or the United Kingdom. Such factors include homogamy (the tendency for people to marry people like themselves, which leads the rich and highly educated to marry one another); the growing importance of money in politics; the "winner-take-all" nature of new technologies in globalized industries; increased automation and use of robots or artificial intelligence; and the prevalence of the financial sector in the countries that have seen the greatest increases in inequality.

It is too early to know the relative importance of these factors in influencing inequality and the shape they will take over the next 20 years. Moreover, they may be offset by still others, such as policy changes in response to a political backlash against rising inequality or the dissipation of economic rents as technologies mature. It therefore seems reasonable to maintain the assumption of unchanged within-country inequality for the advanced economies even in the Kuznets scenario. (The projected Gini index in 2035 under the Kuznets hypothesis for each country is shown in table 3A.1.)

Appendix 3A Household Survey Data Used in the Analysis

The analysis presented in this chapter relies as much as possible on high-quality, internationally comparable survey data on household disposable incomes that are available for many countries through the Luxembourg Income Study (LIS), which covers 64 percent of the world population and 81 percent of world GDP in 2015. The most recent data for the majority of countries in the sample are for 2010–13. For a few countries, data from the early to mid-2000s had to be used instead.

Data for countries that are not in the LIS dataset were obtained from the World Bank's PovcalNet database (http://iresearch.worldbank.org/PovcalNet/), which compiles household surveys, mostly from developing economies. A handful of countries that are in neither the LIS nor the PovcalNet database are captured using data from the World Bank's World Income Inequality Database (WIID) and national accounts.[6] These data are less internationally comparable than the LIS data and combine data on income for some countries with consumption data for others.

Because the World Bank provides only summary statistics (such as the Gini index and decile shares) rather than individual-level microdata, researchers need to make choices about which statistics to use. The analysis in this book approximates a continuous log-normal distribution using the Gini index and the survey mean for each country as inputs.[7,8]

To convert the latest available within-country income distributions to 2015 values, all incomes in the distribution for a given country are increased

---

6. Solt (2014) attempts to standardize the World Bank data to make them more comparable across countries, using multiple imputation techniques. See Jenkins (2014) for a comparison of the unadjusted and standardized World Bank datasets. The global inequality estimates presented here are very similar when these standardized data are used in place of the PovcalNet and WIID data.

7. The log-normal distribution is defined by two parameters, the mean (μ) and the standard deviation (σ), which are related by the following formula: survey mean = $e^{\mu + \frac{1}{2}\sigma^2}$. The Gini index and the standard deviation (σ) of the log-normal distribution are related by the following formula: Gini = $2N\left(\frac{\sigma}{\sqrt{2}}\right) - 1$, where N is the standard normal distribution (see Cowell 2011).

8. An alternative would have been to use the data on decile averages in the PovcalNet database. Doing so would have resulted in a much less granular distribution. For example, a decile of the Indonesian population consisted of about 26 million people in 2015; assigning all of these people identical income would over- or understate the share of East Asia in particular income buckets. In particular, the top decile of the worldwide distribution would be composed exclusively of people living in the advanced economies, because mean income in the top decile in the within-country distributions of the vast majority of emerging-market economies falls well short of the 90th percentile of the global income distribution.

by the rate of growth of the aggregate household final consumption expenditure in the national accounts between the survey year and 2015.[9]

Table 3A.1 displays information about the household survey data used in the analysis as well as data on household final consumption expenditure in the national accounts for each country. These data are used to adjust the survey data as explained in appendix 3B. The Gini index based on the unadjusted survey distribution is also shown alongside the adjusted Gini index. The last column shows the projected adjusted Gini index in 2035, assuming that within-country inequality evolves according to the Kuznets scenario described in the main text.

---

9. In the absence of data on the real growth rate of household disposable incomes, data on the growth of household consumption from national accounts are the best proxy for the countries in the sample.

Table 3A.1 Survey data and inequality measures by country

| Region/country | Household survey | | | HFCE per capita in 2015 (2011) PPP dollars) | Survey mean as percentage of HFCE per capita | Gini index | | Projected Gini index in 2035 under the Kuznets hypothesis |
	Source	Year	Income/ consumption			Unadjusted distribution	Adjusted distribution	
North America								
Canada	LIS	2010	Income	23,400	91.5	33.4	35.7	35.7
Mexico	LIS	2012	Income	9,561	43.2	50.2	70.7	65.4
United States	LIS	2013	Income	36,334	66.3	40.3	53.7	53.7
European Union								
Austria	LIS	2004	Income	22,777	87.3	29.9	34.3	34.3
Belgium	LIS	2000	Income	20,123	85.9	28.5	34.4	34.4
Bulgaria	PovcalNet	2012	Income	9,276	64.3	36.0	49.6	45.0
Croatia	PovcalNet	2011	Income	10,373	62.1	32.0	51.7	47.6
Cyprus	PovcalNet	2012	Income	19,303	51.1	34.3	59.1	59.1
Czech Republic	LIS	2010	Income	13,357	79.6	26.6	34.9	34.9
Denmark	LIS	2010	Income	18,928	102.1	25.2	27.0	27.0
Estonia	LIS	2010	Income	12,342	79.9	32.6	41.1	41.1
Finland	LIS	2013	Income	20,016	90.7	26.9	30.5	30.5
France	LIS	2010	Income	19,933	88.8	31.9	35.8	35.8
Germany	LIS	2010	Income	23,386	85.9	30.2	37.0	37.0
Greece	LIS	2010	Income	15,813	63.8	33.7	46.4	46.4

(table continues)

Table 3A.1 Survey data and inequality measures by country *(continued)*

| Region/country | Household survey | | | HFCE per capita in 2015 (2011 PPP dollars) | Survey mean as percentage of HFCE per capita | Gini index | | Projected Gini index in 2035 under the Kuznets hypothesis |
	Source	Year	Income/ consumption			Unadjusted distribution	Adjusted distribution	
European Union *(continued)*								
Hungary	LIS	2012	Income	11,127	64.2	31.2	48.4	45.3
Ireland	LIS	2010	Income	18,737	85.3	31.8	38.0	38.0
Italy	LIS	2010	Income	19,001	65.3	35.2	49.2	49.2
Latvia	PovcalNet	2012	Income	12,130	60.8	35.5	51.2	49.5
Lithuania	PovcalNet	2012	Income	14,727	55.5	35.2	54.1	54.1
Luxembourg	n.a.	n.a.	n.a.	n.a.	n.a.	n.a.	n.a.	n.a.
Malta	n.a.	n.a.	n.a.	n.a.	n.a.	n.a.	n.a.	n.a.
Netherlands	LIS	2010	Income	19,364	93.6	28.0	31.1	31.1
Poland	LIS	2013	Income	13,929	59.6	34.3	52.2	52.2
Portugal	WIID	2011	Income	16,064	n.a.	34.2	n.a.	n.a.
Romania	PovcalNet	2012	Income	10,695	36.5	34.9	63.3	59.6
Slovak Republic	LIS	2010	Income	13,522	64.6	27.0	42.4	42.4
Slovenia	LIS	2012	Income	13,968	86.5	27.3	31.0	31.0
Spain	LIS	2013	Income	16,680	83.0	36.0	41.5	41.5
Sweden	LIS	2005	Income	20,360	90.8	25.7	29.5	29.5
United Kingdom	LIS	2013	Income	22,983	79.1	34.6	42.7	42.7

Other OECD

Australia	LIS	2010	Income	23,034	90.0	34.2	37.6	37.6
Chile	PovcalNet	2013	Income	12,944	67.9	50.5	58.4	57.9
Iceland	n.a.	n.a.	n.a.	n.a.	n.a.	n.a.	n.a.	n.a.
Israel	LIS	2012	Income	17,251	73.3	41.3	50.5	50.5
Japan	LIS	2008	Income	19,632	75.8	32.1	41.5	41.5
Korea	LIS	2006	Income	15,879	100.0	32.6	34.2	34.2
New Zealand	WIID	2009	Income	19,164	n.a.	31.7	n.a.	n.a.
Norway	LIS	2010	Income	24,318	96.4	25.7	27.5	27.5
Switzerland	LIS	2004	Income	27,243	85.1	31.5	35.9	35.9
Turkey	PovcalNet	2012	Consumption	11,153	56.7	40.2	60.7	57.7
China								
China	LIS	2002	Consumption	4,533	80.6	48.4	56.3	45.0
Hong Kong	WIID	2011	Income	34,332	n.a.	47.5	n.a.	n.a.
Macao	n.a.	n.a.	n.a.	n.a.	n.a.	n.a.	n.a.	n.a.
India	LIS	2011	Income	3,213	64.0	50.0	55.7	51.0

(table continues)

Table 3A.1 Survey data and inequality measures by country *(continued)*

| Region/country | Household survey | | | HFCE per capita in 2015 (2011 PPP dollars) | Survey mean as percentage of HFCE per capita | Gini index | | Projected Gini index in 2035 under the Kuznets hypothesis |
	Source	Year	Income/consumption			Unadjusted distribution	Adjusted distribution	
Latin America and the Caribbean								
Antigua and Barbuda	n.a.	n.a.	n.a.	n.a.	n.a.	n.a.	n.a.	n.a.
Argentina	n.a.	n.a.	n.a.	n.a.	n.a.	n.a.	n.a.	n.a.
Bahamas	n.a.	n.a.	n.a.	n.a.	n.a.	n.a.	n.a.	n.a.
Barbados	n.a.	n.a.	n.a.	n.a.	n.a.	n.a.	n.a.	n.a.
Belize	n.a.	n.a.	n.a.	n.a.	n.a.	n.a.	n.a.	n.a.
Bermuda	n.a.	n.a.	n.a.	n.a.	n.a.	n.a.	n.a.	n.a.
Bolivia	PovcalNet	2013	Income	3,932	132.2	48.1	n.a.	n.a.
Brazil	LIS	2013	Income	7,965	67.6	47.9	57.3	50.6
Colombia	LIS	2013	Income	7,682	52.5	54.8	62.8	54.8
Costa Rica	PovcalNet	2013	Income	9,456	90.1	49.2	n.a.	n.a.
Dominica	n.a.	n.a.	n.a.	n.a.	n.a.	n.a.	n.a.	n.a.
Dominican Republic	LIS	2007	Income	8,781	58.4	52.9	61.7	57.4
Ecuador	PovcalNet	2013	Income	6,075	71.6	47.3	n.a.	n.a.
El Salvador	PovcalNet	2013	Income	7,088	53.7	43.5	56.7	53.7
Grenada	n.a.	n.a.	n.a.	n.a.	n.a.	n.a.	n.a.	n.a.
Guatemala	LIS	2006	Income	5,882	62.9	53.8	60.0	57.9

48

Latin America and the Caribbean

Guyana	n.a.	n.a.	n.a.	n.a.	n.a.	n.a.	n.a.	n.a.
Haiti	PovcalNet	2012	Income	1,526	86.1	60.8	66.4	71.0
Honduras	PovcalNet	2013	Income	3,675	77.8	53.7	62.5	62.1
Jamaica	PovcalNet	2004	Consumption	6,070	68.3	45.5	59.5	57.8
Nicaragua	PovcalNet	2009	Income	3,907	83.1	45.7	n.a.	n.a.
Panama	LIS	2013	Income	10,675	56.8	50.1	63.4	59.6
Paraguay	LIS	2013	Income	5,516	103.6	50.7	53.3	53.3
Peru	LIS	2013	Income	6,888	60.8	46.7	54.6	45.5
Puerto Rico	WIID	2003	Income	16,709	n.a.	55.8	n.a.	n.a.
St. Kitts and Nevis	n.a.	n.a.	n.a.	n.a.	n.a.	n.a.	n.a.	n.a.
St. Lucia	n.a.	n.a.	n.a.	n.a.	n.a.	n.a.	n.a.	n.a.
St. Vincent and the Grenadines	n.a.	n.a.	n.a.	n.a.	n.a.	n.a.	n.a.	n.a.
Suriname	n.a.	n.a.	n.a.	n.a.	n.a.	n.a.	n.a.	n.a.
Uruguay	LIS	2013	Income	12,513	63.4	40.6	54.2	53.1
Venezuela	PovcalNet	2006	Income	8,434	55.4	46.9	58.4	51.5

(table continues)

Table 3A.1 Survey data and inequality measures by country *(continued)*

| Region/country | Household survey | | | | Survey mean as percentage of HFCE per capita | Gini index | | | Projected Gini index in 2035 under the Kuznets hypothesis |
	Source	Year	Income/ consumption	HFCE per capita in 2015 (2011 PPP dollars)		Unadjusted distribution	Adjusted distribution	
East Asia and the Pacific								
Brunei Darussalam	n.a.	n.a.	n.a.	n.a.	n.a.	n.a.	n.a.	n.a.
Cambodia	PovcalNet	2011	Consumption	2,260	71.7	31.8	47.2	45.0
Fiji	n.a.	n.a.	n.a.	n.a.	n.a.	n.a.	n.a.	n.a.
Indonesia	PovcalNet	2010	Consumption	5,060	37.8	35.6	69.1	59.8
Kiribati	n.a.	n.a.	n.a.	n.a.	n.a.	n.a.	n.a.	n.a.
Lao	PovcalNet	2012	Consumption	3,150	47.4	36.2	64.1	58.6
Malaysia	PovcalNet	2009	Income	11,973	86.2	46.3	n.a.	n.a.
Marshall Islands	n.a.	n.a.	n.a.	n.a.	n.a.	n.a.	n.a.	n.a.
Micronesia	n.a.	n.a.	n.a.	n.a.	n.a.	n.a.	n.a.	n.a.
Mongolia	PovcalNet	2012	Consumption	5,803	79.2	33.8	44.4	44.4
Palau	n.a.	n.a.	n.a.	n.a.	n.a.	n.a.	n.a.	n.a.
Papua New Guinea	PovcalNet	2009	Consumption	1,372	105.1	43.9	n.a.	n.a.
Philippines	PovcalNet	2012	Consumption	4,731	49.8	43.0	66.9	55.7
Samoa	n.a.	n.a.	n.a.	n.a.	n.a.	n.a.	n.a.	n.a.
Singapore	WIID	2012	Income	21,476	n.a.	47.8	n.a.	n.a.

East Asia and the Pacific

Solomon Islands	n.a.	n.a.	n.a.	n.a.	n.a.	n.a.	n.a.
Taiwan	LIS	2013	Income	23,516	72.3	32.4	42.3	42.3
Thailand	PovcalNet	2012	Consumption	7,598	72.0	39.3	52.6	45.0
Timor-Leste	PovcalNet	2007	Consumption	1,448	87.6	31.6	38.6	43.4
Tonga	n.a.	n.a.	n.a.	n.a.	n.a.	n.a.	n.a.
Tuvalu	n.a.	n.a.	n.a.	n.a.	n.a.	n.a.	n.a.
Vanuatu	n.a.	n.a.	n.a.	n.a.	n.a.	n.a.	n.a.
Vietnam	PovcalNet	2012	Consumption	3,376	103.2	38.7	n.a.	n.a.

South Asia

Afghanistan	WIID	2007	Consumption	1,623	n.a.	29.0	n.a.	n.a.
Bangladesh	PovcalNet	2010	Consumption	2,048	58.8	32.1	54.8	55.7
Bhutan	n.a.	n.a.	n.a.	n.a.	n.a.	n.a.	n.a.
Maldives	n.a.	n.a.	n.a.	n.a.	n.a.	n.a.	n.a.
Nepal	PovcalNet	2010	Consumption	1,786	97.1	32.8	34.7	37.7
Pakistan	PovcalNet	2011	Consumption	3,617	43.4	29.6	62.0	61.4
Sri Lanka	PovcalNet	2012	Consumption	7,211	41.8	38.6	68.1	63.5

(table continues)

Table 3A.1 Survey data and inequality measures by country (*continued*)

| Region/country | Household survey | | | HFCE per capita in 2015 (2011 PPP dollars) | Survey mean as percentage of HFCE per capita | Gini index | | Projected Gini index in 2035 under the Kuznets hypothesis |
	Source	Year	Income/ consumption			Unadjusted distribution	Adjusted distribution	
Middle East and North Africa								
Algeria	n.a.	n.a.	n.a.	n.a.	n.a.	n.a.	n.a.	n.a.
Bahrain	n.a.	n.a.	n.a.	n.a.	n.a.	n.a.	n.a.	n.a.
Djibouti	n.a.	n.a.	n.a.	n.a.	n.a.	n.a.	n.a.	n.a.
Egypt	LIS	2012	Income	7,355	35.6	51.8	75.4	69.7
Iran	PovcalNet	2013	Consumption	6,523	93.4	37.4	40.7	40.7
Iraq	PovcalNet	2012	Consumption	6,950	41.0	29.5	63.1	54.1
Jordan	PovcalNet	2010	Consumption	7,769	84.8	33.7	41.4	41.4
Lebanon	WIID	2004	Consumption	10,923	n.a.	37.0	n.a.	n.a.
Libya	n.a.	n.a.	n.a.	n.a.	n.a.	n.a.	n.a.	n.a.
Morocco	PovcalNet	2007	Consumption	3,837	94.9	40.7	43.4	43.4
Oman	n.a.	n.a.	n.a.	n.a.	n.a.	n.a.	n.a.	n.a.
Qatar	n.a.	n.a.	n.a.	n.a.	n.a.	n.a.	n.a.	n.a.
Saudi Arabia	n.a.	n.a.	n.a.	n.a.	n.a.	n.a.	n.a.	n.a.
Tunisia	PovcalNet	2010	Consumption	6,630	66.1	35.8	52.9	48.2
United Arab Emirates	n.a.	n.a.	n.a.	n.a.	n.a.	n.a.	n.a.	n.a.
West Bank and Gaza	n.a.	n.a.	n.a.	n.a.	n.a.	n.a.	n.a.	n.a.
Yemen	PovcalNet	2005	Consumption	2,520	102.2	35.9	n.a.	n.a.

Sub-Saharan Africa

Angola	PovcalNet	2009	Consumption	2,845	54.4	42.7	64.7	63.9
Benin	PovcalNet	2012	Consumption	1,253	81.6	43.4	52.8	57.4
Botswana	PovcalNet	2009	Consumption	5,660	74.8	60.5	68.9	64.8
Burkina Faso	PovcalNet	2009	Consumption	696	94.6	39.8	43.7	56.8
Burundi	PovcalNet	2006	Consumption	467	128.5	33.4	n.a.	n.a.
Cabo Verde	n.a.	n.a.	n.a.	n.a.	n.a.	n.a.	n.a.	n.a.
Cameroon	PovcalNet	2007	Consumption	2,233	80.6	42.8	52.3	53.6
Central African Republic	PovcalNet	2008	Consumption	480	117.7	56.2	n.a.	n.a.
Chad	PovcalNet	2011	Consumption	1,349	93.4	43.3	47.2	50.0
Comoros	n.a.	n.a.	n.a.	n.a.	n.a.	n.a.	n.a.	n.a.
Congo, Democratic Republic of	PovcalNet	2012	Consumption	546	117.7	42.1	n.a.	n.a.
Congo, Republic of	PovcalNet	2011	Consumption	1,652	71.7	40.2	54.5	57.1
Côte d'Ivoire	PovcalNet	2008	Consumption	2,381	82.2	43.2	51.8	52.4
Equatorial Guinea	n.a.	n.a.	n.a.	n.a.	n.a.	n.a.	n.a.	n.a.
Eritrea	n.a.	n.a.	n.a.	n.a.	n.a.	n.a.	n.a.	n.a.

(table continues)

Table 3A.1 Survey data and inequality measures by country *(continued)*

| Region/country | Household survey | | | | Survey mean as percentage of HFCE per capita | Gini index | | Projected Gini index in 2035 under the Kuznets hypothesis |
	Source	Year	Income/ consumption	HFCE per capita in 2015 (2011 PPP dollars)		Unadjusted distribution	Adjusted distribution	
Sub-Saharan Africa *(continued)*								
Ethiopia	PovcalNet	2011	Consumption	844	137.6	33.2	n.a.	n.a.
Gabon	PovcalNet	2005	Consumption	4,819	72.1	42.2	55.3	54.3
Gambia	PovcalNet	2003	Consumption	1,228	101.8	47.3	n.a.	n.a.
Ghana	PovcalNet	2006	Consumption	1,824	96.5	42.8	45.0	47.8
Guinea	PovcalNet	2012	Consumption	973	104.0	33.7	n.a.	n.a.
Guinea-Bissau	PovcalNet	2012	Consumption	1,035	82.6	50.7	59.1	64.3
Kenya	PovcalNet	2005	Consumption	2,271	86.7	48.5	54.7	55.9
Lesotho	PovcalNet	2010	Consumption	2,321	41.8	54.2	78.0	77.6
Liberia	PovcalNet	2007	Consumption	1,184	51.3	36.5	63.0	70.5
Madagascar	PovcalNet	2010	Consumption	1,086	45.4	40.6	69.3	77.6
Malawi	PovcalNet	2010	Consumption	936	88.7	46.1	52.3	56.7
Mali	PovcalNet	2010	Consumption	1,574	72.1	33.0	48.2	48.6
Mauritania	PovcalNet	2008	Consumption	1,644	129.0	37.5	n.a.	n.a.
Mauritius	PovcalNet	2012	Consumption	11,494	39.8	35.8	67.3	64.7
Mozambique	PovcalNet	2009	Consumption	754	98.5	45.6	47.5	62.6
Namibia	PovcalNet	2010	Consumption	6,050	58.3	61.0	74.9	71.9

Sub-Saharan Africa

Niger	PovcalNet	2011	Consumption	589	148.5	31.5	n.a.	n.a.
Nigeria	PovcalNet	2010	Consumption	3,648	26.8	43.0	79.8	74.0
Rwanda	PovcalNet	2011	Consumption	1,364	87.5	51.3	57.3	63.0
São Tomé and Príncipe	n.a.	n.a.	n.a.	n.a.	n.a.	n.a.	n.a.	n.a.
Senegal	PovcalNet	2011	Consumption	1,637	72.3	40.3	54.3	57.9
Seychelles	n.a.	n.a.	n.a.	n.a.	n.a.	n.a.	n.a.	n.a.
Sierra Leone	PovcalNet	2011	Consumption	1,258	72.1	34.0	49.2	56.3
South Africa	LIS	2012	Income	7,068	61.7	65.0	75.1	66.3
Sudan	PovcalNet	2009	Consumption	2,130	92.0	35.4	39.8	41.2
Swaziland	PovcalNet	2010	Consumption	6,269	18.1	51.5	n.a.	n.a.
Tanzania	PovcalNet	2012	Consumption	1,384	75.5	37.8	50.7	55.7
Togo	PovcalNet	2011	Consumption	1,436	96.5	46.0	48.3	52.0
Trinidad and Tobago	n.a.	n.a.	n.a.	n.a.	n.a.	n.a.	n.a.	n.a.
Uganda	PovcalNet	2012	Consumption	1,192	112.3	42.4	n.a.	n.a.
Zambia	PovcalNet	2010	Consumption	2,218	47.3	55.6	76.5	77.7
Zimbabwe	WIID	2011	Consumption	1,469	n.a.	42.3	n.a.	n.a.

(table continues)

Table 3A.1 Survey data and inequality measures by country (*continued*)

| Region/country | Household survey | | | | Survey mean as percentage of HFCE per capita | Gini index | | Projected Gini index in 2035 under the Kuznets hypothesis |
	Source	Year	Income/ consumption	HFCE per capita in 2015 (2011 PPP dollars)		Unadjusted distribution	Adjusted distribution	
Eastern Europe and Central Asia								
Albania	PovcalNet	2012	Consumption	6,263	45.3	29.0	60.0	52.0
Armenia	PovcalNet	2013	Consumption	5,807	34.6	31.5	68.7	58.3
Azerbaijan	PovcalNet	2005	Consumption	6,805	82.6	16.6	26.5	26.5
Belarus	PovcalNet	2012	Consumption	10,144	77.0	26.0	38.4	38.4
Bosnia and Herzegovina	PovcalNet	2007	Consumption	6,913	113.5	33.0	n.a.	n.a.
Georgia	LIS	2013	Income	6,334	45.1	40.8	62.3	52.6
Kazakhstan	PovcalNet	2013	Consumption	9,964	42.4	26.4	59.8	55.0
Kyrgyz Republic	PovcalNet	2012	Consumption	2,883	69.2	27.4	44.6	44.6
Macedonia	PovcalNet	2008	Consumption	7,429	59.8	44.1	62.3	59.1
Moldova	PovcalNet	2013	Consumption	4,416	80.1	28.5	39.3	39.3
Montenegro	n.a.	n.a.	n.a.	n.a.	n.a.	n.a.	n.a.	n.a.
Russia	LIS	2013	Income	12,643	66.6	32.5	45.6	45.0
Serbia	LIS	2013	Income	7,805	54.2	34.3	54.9	49.9
Tajikistan	PovcalNet	2009	Consumption	2,186	104.1	30.8	n.a.	n.a.
Turkmenistan	n.a.	n.a.	n.a.	n.a.	n.a.	n.a.	n.a.	n.a.
Ukraine	PovcalNet	2013	Consumption	6,342	77.4	24.6	37.0	37.0
Uzbekistan	PovcalNet	2003	Consumption	2,665	54.3	35.3	59.6	60.0

HFCE = household final consumption expenditure; PPP = purchasing power parity; n.a. = not available; WIID = World Income Inequality Database; LIS = Luxembourg Income Study

Appendix 3B Methodology for Adjusting the Data

This appendix (1) documents the size of the gap between household surveys and national accounts data in their measurement of income or consumption for each country in the LIS sample; (2) provides new evidence that the size of the gap is correlated with proxies for inequality, the size of the informal economy, tax evasion, and corruption, suggesting underreporting of incomes and undersampling of rich households; (3) discusses the severity of these problems across different types of income; and (4) explains how the survey data were adjusted to close the gap with national accounts. The impact of the adjustment is reported for individual countries both to provide a transparent account of the methodology and because it may be of interest in its own right.

Gap between Household Survey and National Accounts Data

Chapter 3 provides a novel approach to reconciling the differences between income and consumption data from household surveys and average values based on aggregate data reported in national accounts—an issue that has long challenged researchers. The national aggregate used is household final consumption expenditure (HFCE). This measure was chosen for two reasons. First, much of this book is concerned with household consumption and its composition, as measured in household surveys. HFCE is the corresponding concept in the national accounts. Second, HFCE is a more appropriate aggregate to scale up than GDP, which significantly overstates household resources because it includes items such as depreciation, retained earnings of corporations, and government revenues, which are not distributed back to households as cash transfers (Anand and Segal 2008). In the United States, for example, disposable personal income was 75 percent of GDP in 2015, according to the Bureau of Economic Analysis. Although the United States and a few other countries report personal disposable income in their national accounts, most countries do not. HFCE is a reasonable proxy that is widely available for global analysis.

The gap between survey data and national accounts in the LIS sample of countries ranges from 0 or less (in Paraguay, Denmark, China, and Korea) to more than 50 percent (in Georgia, Mexico, and Egypt) (figure 3B.1). The gap tends to be smallest in the advanced economies, larger in transition economies and in Southern Europe, and largest in emerging-market economies (an important exception is China, where the saving rate is unusually high).

Household surveys and national accounts yield different results because they define the measure (income or consumption) differently and are subject to different sources of measurement errors and omissions (Deaton 2005). If

Figure 3B.1 Mean income from household surveys as percent of household final consumption expenditure in the national accounts

percent

Note: The figure is based on the most recent data available for each country.

Sources: Luxembourg Income Study for household survey data on income distribution; World Bank national accounts data for household final consumption expenditure.

the household saving rate is positive, mean income should be higher than mean consumption. The fact that the survey mean income is actually significantly lower than the national accounts measure of household consumption in most countries suggests important differences in definitional and measurement issues between household surveys and national accounts.[10]

Deaton (2005) notes three important differences between the ways surveys and national accounts define consumption:

- HFCE includes the imputed rent from owner-occupied housing, which surveys almost always exclude.

- HFCE includes an estimate of the consumption value of financial intermediation, known as FISIM (financial intermediation services indirectly measured). FISIM is measured as the difference between the interest paid to banks and other intermediaries and the interest paid by them. Household surveys include no corresponding measure.

- HFCE includes consumption by nonprofit institutions serving households, such as charities and nongovernmental organizations. Adjusting the national accounts measure to exclude these items is often impossible, because for most countries the necessary disaggregation is not available to assess how important these definitional differences are in driving the gap.

Both surveys and national accounts are prone to measurement errors and omissions. Survey results are distorted if failure to participate differs according to household characteristics. Better-off households are less likely to respond to surveys, for example, leading to a truncation of the survey sample (Groves and Couper 1998; Székely and Hilgert 1999; Korinek, Mistiaen, and Ravallion 2006). National accounts are less vulnerable to this problem, because they track money rather than people and are therefore more likely to capture large transactions (Deaton 2005). Income surveys also suffer from underreporting by survey respondents. The scale of underreporting is likely to differ across different types of income.

Estimating HFCE in the national accounts is subject to its own measurement problems. It is measured as a residual of aggregate production after subtracting estimates of consumption by government and firms. There is no guarantee that any errors in the estimation of these three aggregates will be mutually offsetting (e.g., overestimate of production offsetting an overestimate of government and firm consumption, leaving the

10. By coincidence, in China the effect of the exceptionally high household saving rate on the gap almost exactly offsets these other definitional and measurement issues, so that the mean survey income is nearly equal to HFCE per capita measured in the national accounts.

Figure 3B.2 Relationship between inequality and gap between mean income reported in household surveys and household final consumption expenditure in the national accounts

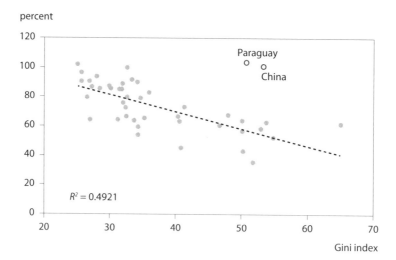

Note: The figure is based on the most recent data available for each country. The y-axis shows mean consumption from household surveys as percent of household final consumption expenditure. Paraguay and China are excluded from the calculation of the best-fitting line, because they are outliers.

Sources: Luxembourg Income Study for household survey data on income distribution; World Bank national accounts data for household final consumption expenditure.

residual correctly measured). It is possible that instead the measurement errors will compound the error in measuring household consumption (Deaton 2005, Anand and Segal 2008).

Correlation between Size of the Gap and Proxies for Inequality and Institutional Quality

Empirical results on a cross section of countries in the LIS sample suggest that measurement errors in household surveys explain a significant portion of the gap between surveys and national accounts. Figure 3B.2 shows a negative, statistically significant relationship between the ratio of the survey mean to HFCE per capita and the Gini index based on the LIS data.[11] This

11. Deaton (2005) fails to find such a relationship in a larger sample of countries in the World Bank database. This difference probably reflects the fact that the results presented here are based on better-quality, internationally harmonized data from the LIS.

Figure 3B.3 Relationship between perceptions of corruption and gap between income reported in household surveys and household final consumption expenditure in the national accounts

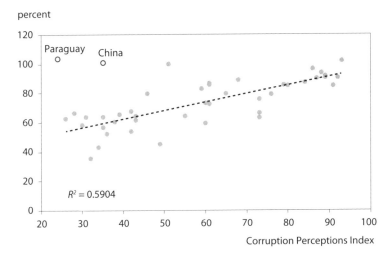

percent

Note: The figure is based on the most recent data available for each country. The y-axis shows mean consumption from household surveys as a percent of household final consumption expenditure. Higher values of the Corruption Perceptions Index indicate lower perception of corruption. Paraguay and China are excluded from the calculation of the best fit line because they are extreme outliers.

Sources: Luxembourg Income Study for household survey data on income distribution; World Bank national accounts data for household final consumption expenditure; Transparency International for the Corruption Perceptions Index.

relationship is consistent with truncation of the survey sample at the top of the distribution of individual incomes. One would expect that more unequal countries, where the share of income going to the top few percent is very large, would have a wider gap between survey mean income and HFCE if those top few percent are underrepresented in the survey.[12] Although this evidence is by no means conclusive, it is suggestive of a link between top income shares and the degree to which surveys understate total and mean income.

The gap between surveys and national accounts is also correlated with Transparency International's Corruption Perceptions Index (on which a higher value indicates lower perception of corruption) (figure 3B.3). The

---

12. The extent of truncation also depends on the quality of the survey design, the sampling procedure, and the methodology for imputing nonreported incomes. As a result of these differences, the share of the population that is unrepresented or underrepresented in the survey varies widely across countries.

Table 3B.1 Ordinary least squares regression results of survey mean as percent of household final consumption expenditure per capita

Item	(1)	(2)	(3)
Gini index	−1.156 (−6.23)		−0.578 (−2.87)
Corruption Perceptions Index		0.580 (7.59)	0.409 (5.95)
R^2	0.49	0.59	0.66
Number of observations	42	42	42

Note: All coefficients are significant at the 1 percent level. t-statistics are shown in parentheses. Paraguay and China are excluded from the regression because they are outliers.

index can be considered a proxy for the quality of institutions—and more generally the level of trust and honesty in dealings between citizens and their government—which may influence the propensity to evade tax and the honesty with which some survey respondents answer questions about their household incomes. Together the Gini index and the Corruption Perceptions Index explain two-thirds of the variation in the gap between surveys and national accounts across countries (table 3B.1, column 3).[13]

Measurement Error in Income Surveys

Evidence from psychology and economics suggests that the degree of underreporting in income surveys varies with the type of income (wages and salaries, self-employment, transfers, or capital). Drawing on an extensive review of studies in cognitive and social psychology, John Bound, Charles Brown, and Nancy Mathiowetz (2001) highlight three factors associated with measurement error in income survey responses:

- Cognitive effort: The accuracy of response is likely to be a function of the saliency of the information requested and the complexity of the mental process needed to retrieve it from memory.

- Social desirability: Socially undesirable behavior and outcomes tend to be underreported, and socially desirable behavior and outcomes tend to be overreported.

---

13. Omitted factors associated with the degree of economic development do not appear to drive the strength of this relationship. When the logarithm of per capita GDP is added as an explanatory variable, its coefficient is not statistically significant at the 5 percent level, whereas the coefficient on the Corruption Perceptions Index remains significant at the 5 percent level.

- Risk of self-incrimination: Despite the absence of penalties for misreporting income in household surveys, respondents who believe that survey responses may be shared with the tax authorities are less likely to respond truthfully.

This section examines measurement error in four sources of income: wages and salaries, self-employment, transfers, and capital.[14] The analysis shows that both the degree of measurement error and the relative importance of misreporting and sample truncation vary significantly by type of income. Household surveys do a good job of capturing wages and salaries but understate income from self-employment, nonpension social transfers, and capital.

Wages and Salaries

Recalling one's wage or salary accurately is likely to involve less cognitive effort than recalling income from other sources, for several reasons. First, for the average employee, earnings are the most important and stable source of income. Second, wages or salary are a significant part of many people's self-identity. Third, retrieval of this information is required many times a year—during the annual pay round, in the preparation of tax returns, in the completion of applications for credit cards and loans. In addition, because employers usually deduct income taxes and social security contributions from gross earnings, there is less scope to misreport this source of income to the tax authorities and therefore less incentive to underreport it in income surveys.

Estimates of annual earnings are subject to relatively small levels of response error, according to micro-level validation studies that compare individual survey responses with employers' records or tax/social security records (Bound, Brown, and Mathiowetz 2001). To the extent that misreporting by survey participants occurs, people with relatively low earnings tend to overreport whereas people with relatively high earnings tend to underreport. If society views both poverty and wealth with moral suspicion, social desirability bias could be driving this pattern. These findings indicate that undersampling of high-earnings households is much more important than underreporting as the source of the gap between surveys and national accounts with respect to wages and salaries.

14. In most countries in the LIS data, wages and salaries represent the most significant source of income (63 percent on average). The average share of income from transfers (20 percent) exceeds the average income share of income from self-employment (14 percent) in most countries. Income from capital is the smallest component in most countries (3 percent). (Different degrees of underreporting across different types of income may distort these shares.)

If measurement error were uncorrelated with the level of wages, greater measurement error would lead to higher measured inequality. The observed reversion to the mean, however, makes the impact of measurement error on inequality estimates ambiguous. Peter Gottschalk and Minh Huynh (2010) show that in the United States the variance is lower in survey data than in administrative data, suggesting that measurement error in surveys leads to underestimating inequality.

Macro-level validation, which compares aggregate earnings in household surveys with the corresponding aggregates in the national accounts, confirms that misreporting of wages and salaries is limited. In most advanced economies, the gap is less than 20 percent.[15]

Income from Self-Employment

Obtaining accurate information on the incomes of the self-employed is likely to be more challenging than obtaining accurate information on wages and salaries, for two reasons. First, the self-employed have greater scope to hide part of their income from the tax authorities and may have an incentive to keep the income they report in the survey consistent with that which they declare on their tax returns, to avoid self-incrimination. Second, income from self-employment is likely to be less stable and more difficult to calculate than wage and salary income. Recalling the number reported to the tax authorities may be easier than calculating an accurate one.

Studies show that the self-employed significantly underreport their income in surveys. Validation analysis cannot make use of administrative data, such as tax returns, because underreporting often reflects income hidden from the tax authorities, as confirmed by random audits by the Internal Revenue Service in the United States. Instead, researchers use a method pioneered by Christopher A. Pissarides and Guglielmo Weber (1989) in which they first estimate the relationship between expenditures (for which incentives to underreport are smaller) and income for a sample of wage and salary workers and then use the estimated coefficients from this relationship to predict the income of the self-employed based on their reported level of expenditures.

The results indicate that self-employed households underreport their income by 10–60 percent, depending on the country. There is also evidence that underreporting rises with the number of self-employed individuals in a household (Johansson 2005); that unincorporated businesses underreport more than incorporated ones (Engström and Holmlund 2009); and that

---

15. These results are based on the authors' calculations comparing mean wages and salaries in the LIS data with the wages and salaries aggregate in the national accounts. More detail and results for individual countries are available from the authors upon request.

self-employed people in blue-collar occupations underreport more than self-employed people in white-collar ones (Pissarides and Weber 1989).

Comparison between income from self-employment in the surveys and mixed income (defined as the surplus or deficit accruing from production by unincorporated enterprises owned by households) in the national accounts confirms that the discrepancy is much larger than the discrepancy for wages and salaries for most countries for which data are available. Indeed, the figure exceeds 40 percent in most countries. The large gap likely reflects not only underreporting but also the fact that self-employment income is distributed more unequally than wages and salaries, resulting in a greater sample truncation.[16]

Income from Social Transfers

The accuracy of survey data on income from social transfers is likely to vary by type of benefit. Survey respondents are more likely to accurately report relatively stable and permanent transfers, such as pensions and disability insurance, than more complex or transitory transfers, such as unemployment benefits. Some societies may stigmatize some benefits, such as food stamps, leading to underreporting. Evidence for the United States reveals significant downward bias in survey estimates of transfer income, particularly nonpension transfer income (Bound, Brown, and Mathiowetz 2001; Meyer, Mok, and Sullivan 2015).

Income from Capital

Both theoretical considerations and back-of-the-envelope calculations suggest that the gap between survey and national accounts data on capital income is likely to be sizable, because of both underreporting and, especially, sample truncation. Survey data on capital income are especially vulnerable to sample truncation because income from assets is much more concentrated than labor income (OECD 2015a). Moreover, financial wealth is significantly more concentrated than nonfinancial (largely housing) wealth. For these reasons, failure to capture the richest households in the LIS data is the most likely explanation for the size of the gap in capital income reported in surveys and recorded in national accounts. Underreporting may also be greater than for wages and salaries because income from capital is more volatile and therefore more difficult to recall than wage and salary income.[17]

---

16. Details are available from the authors upon request.

17. The only micro-level validation study of capital income (Grondin and Michaud 1994) finds that more than a fifth of survey respondents who reported capital income on their

Adjusting Survey Data to Close the Gap between Surveys and National Accounts

The adjustment used in this book to close the gap between survey means and national account aggregates consists of correcting survey data for both underreporting of income and sample truncation, to a differing extent depending on each source of income. It increases self-employment income to account for underreporting and shifts some of the density into the upper tail of the distribution of total income to account for sample truncation across all income sources. (Data constraints do not allow adjustments to be made for the underreporting of social transfers.[18])

The distributional data come from a variety of sources (income surveys for some countries and consumption surveys for others, microdata for some countries but not for others). The methodology of adjustment is therefore tailored based on the availability of data, using the decision tree shown in figure 3B.4.

This approach increases self-employment income reported in the survey to correct for underreporting; it does not adjust consumption surveys, in which underreporting is less prevalent. Where microdata are available, the adjustment is applied to self-employment income directly. As a result, mean income usually increases, and inequality changes, depending on the joint distribution of self-employment income and income from other sources. Where microdata are not available, the mean of the distribution is increased based on the estimated relationship for the sample of countries with microdata, leaving the distribution of incomes around the mean unchanged. China is a special case, because of its unusually high household saving rate, which makes use of income data inappropriate. Consumption microdata, drawn from the LIS database, are used instead.

Any remaining gap between the survey mean and HFCE per capita (after adjusting for underreporting by the self-employed in the case of income data and all of the gap in the consumption data) is eliminated by adjusting the upper tail of the distribution. This adjustment is motivated

---

tax returns reported zero capital income in surveys; another fifth reported an amount that differed from the tax data by more than 5 percent. Studies looking at asset ownership confirm significant nonreporting of savings accounts and stock ownership (Bound, Brown, and Mathiowetz 2001).

18. The underreporting of social transfers is likely to lead to an upward bias in inequality estimates, because most recipients of social transfers are in the lower part of the income distribution. This problem is greater in advanced economies than in emerging-market economies, where the welfare state is less developed. The bias is unlikely to be large, however, because pensions account for two-thirds of all social transfer payments on average in advanced economies, and the problem of underreporting tends to be smaller for pensions than other types of transfer income.

Figure 3B.4   Adjustment method used to close the gap between survey means and household final consumption expenditure in the national accounts

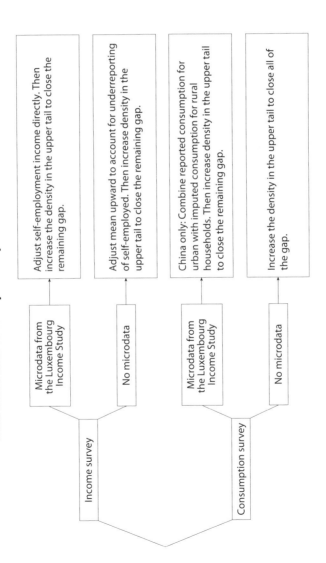

Income survey

- Microdata from the Luxembourg Income Study → Adjust self-employment income directly. Then increase the density in the upper tail to close the remaining gap.

- No microdata → Adjust mean upward to account for underreporting of self-employed. Then increase density in the upper tail to close the remaining gap.

Consumption survey

- Microdata from the Luxembourg Income Study → China only: Combine reported consumption for urban with imputed consumption for rural households. Then increase density in the upper tail to close the remaining gap.

- No microdata → Increase the density in the upper tail to close all of the gap.

by the need to adjust for both underreporting by and undersampling of rich households in the surveys, across all types of income.

Adjustment for Underreporting of Self-Employment Income

Adjustment for underreporting of self-employment income is greater the lower the value of Transparency International's Corruption Perceptions Index, a proxy for the size of the informal economy and the prevalence of tax evasion (lower values indicate higher perceptions of corruption). This information is available for almost all countries. It is preferred over alternatives, such as Friedrich Schneider's measure of the shadow economy (Schneider and Enste 2013), because it is more closely correlated with a measure of the nonobserved economy derived from national accounts that is available for a smaller subset of countries (United Nations 2008, Gyomai and van de Ven 2014).

The Corruption Perceptions Index is also correlated with measures of underreporting by self-employed households estimated in micro-based validation studies for eight countries (figure 3B.5).[19] The line of best fit is estimated using a population-weighted regression for this small cross section.

Adjustment Method for Countries in the Luxembourg Income Study

Self-employment incomes in the LIS microdata for all countries in the sample except China are scaled up depending on each country's susceptibility to tax evasion (proxied by the Corruption Perceptions Index in the survey year), using the estimated coefficient from the population-weighted regression in figure 3B.5. The factor by which self-employment incomes in the survey is multiplied is thus country specific but common to all households with self-employment income within a country.

The effect of the adjustment on the survey mean also depends on the share of self-employment income in total income. This share varies considerably across countries (figure 3B.6).

The adjustment closes a significant portion of the gap between mean income in household surveys and the national accounts measure of HFCE

---

19. The headline results in these studies relate to underreporting of total income by households categorized as self-employed. To define self-employment, some studies use the self-reported status of the household head; others use a threshold for the share of self-employment income in total household income. To make the estimates consistent, it is assumed that underreporting occurs only on the self-employment portion of income and that wage income is reported accurately. Estimates of the share of self-employment income in total household income for those households classified as self-employed (obtained from the LIS using definitions of self-employment consistent with those used in each study) are used to compute the underreporting of self-employment income necessary to generate the results for total income reported by each study.

Figure 3B.5   Relationship between underreporting of self-employment income and institutional quality

percent of self-employment income underreported

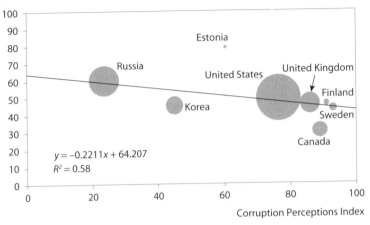

Note: The size of the bubbles is proportional to population.

Sources: Data on underreporting of self-employment income are from the following sources: Canada: Schuetze (2002); Estonia: Kukk and Staehr (2013); Finland: Johansson (2005); Russia and Korea: Kim, Gibson, and Chung (2009); Sweden: Engström and Holmlund (2009); United Kingdom: Pissarides and Weber (1989); United States: Hurst, Li, and Pugsley (2010). The Corruption Perceptions Index data are from Transparency International.

per capita in many economies (figure 3B.7). It is usually larger in emerging-market economies, which tend to have a larger share of self-employment income in total income and a larger informal economy and therefore greater underreporting of self-employment income.

Some advanced economies, particularly the United States and several countries in Eastern and Central Europe, are exceptions to this pattern. In these countries, the gaps between the survey and national accounts data are large and the adjustment closes only a small portion of the gap, because self-employment rates are low by international standards and Corruption Perceptions Indexes are relatively high (indicating low perception of corruption).

Adjustment to self-employment income also affects the Gini index. The precise effect depends on the joint distribution of self-employment income and income from other sources, notably wages and salaries. The adjustment raises the Gini index in all countries except Estonia, Slovenia, and Georgia, with the largest upward revisions in Italy, the Czech Republic, and Greece (figure 3B.8).

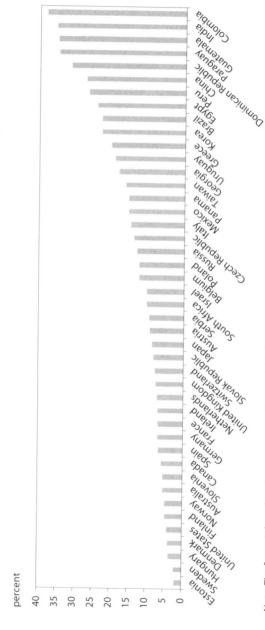

70

Figure 3B.6 Income from self-employment as percent of total household income

percent

Note: The figure is based on the most recent data available for each country.

Source: Luxembourg Income Study.

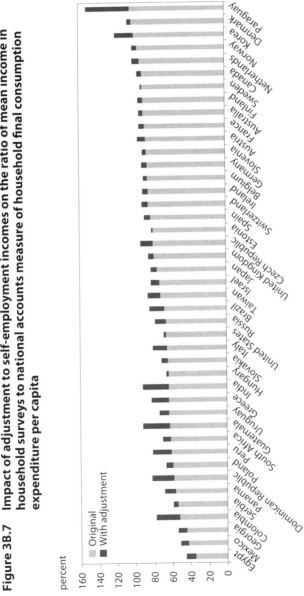

Figure 3B.7   Impact of adjustment to self-employment incomes on the ratio of mean income in household surveys to national accounts measure of household final consumption expenditure per capita

Note: The figure is based on the most recent data available for each country.

Sources: Luxembourg Income Study for household survey data on disposable income; World Bank national accounts data for household final consumption expenditure.

Figure 3B.8 Impact of adjustment to self-employment incomes on within-country inequality

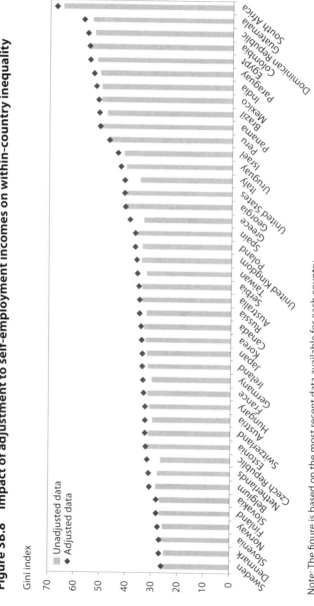

Gini index

Note: The figure is based on the most recent data available for each country.

Source: Luxembourg Income Study.

Adjustment Method for Countries Not Included in the Luxembourg Income Study

For the 12 countries in the World Bank PovcalNet database for which aggregate information on survey means and the Gini index come from household income surveys, the absence of microdata means that it is not possible to adjust self-employment income directly. In these cases, the mean of the distribution is adjusted based on the relationships observed in the LIS data. Specifically, for the cross section of 39 countries with LIS data, the change in mean household income stemming from the adjustment outlined in the previous section is regressed on the Corruption Perceptions Index as well as total employment and the self-employment share in total employment from the LIS data. All of the coefficients are statistically significant, with the expected signs (table 3B.2). The three regressors jointly account for 90 percent of the variation in the dependent variable.

The survey means for the non-LIS income-based countries are then adjusted by applying the estimated coefficients from table 3B.1 to their Corruption Perceptions Index, total employment, and self-employment share. The adjustment brings the survey means closer to HFCE per capita, although in five cases (in Latin America and Malaysia) the adjustment causes the survey mean to exceed HFCE per capita (figure 3B.9).[20,21] For these countries HFCE per capita is used in place of the adjusted survey mean, and no further adjustment (to the upper tail of the distribution) is made.

Adjustment of the Upper Tail of the Distribution

The remaining gap between the survey mean and HFCE per capita is eliminated by shifting the distribution density toward the upper tail of the distribution of total income by splicing a thicker upper tail onto the distributions obtained from survey data (adjusted for underreporting of self-employment income where appropriate) in a smooth and continuous fashion. The thicker tail follows the Pareto distribution. The Pareto coef-

---

20. The adjusted survey mean exceeds HFCE per capita in these countries because the initial gap is relatively small. The fact that similar countries for which better data are available (in the LIS) show large gaps suggests that the original survey means may have been too high.

21. No clear relationship was found between the change in the Gini index as a result of the adjustment of self-employment income and aggregate variables available for the non-LIS countries. The effect of the adjustment on the Gini index depends on the joint distribution of self-employment income and wage income: their respective means, inequality in each, and the degree of overlap between the two distributions. This kind of information comes only from microdata; no useful proxies are available for non-LIS countries. The Gini indices in the non-LIS sample are therefore not adjusted to reflect the underreporting of self-employment incomes.

Table 3B.2 Cross-country regression results of adjustment in the ratio of mean income in household surveys to national accounts measure of household final consumption expenditure per capita

Item	Coefficient	t-statistic
Self-employment share	0.52	8.94
Corruption Perceptions Index	-0.22	-5.29
Employment	0.27	2.83
R^2		0.9
Number of observations		39

ficient, which determines the thickness of the tail, is chosen to ensure that the mean of the resulting joint distribution equals HFCE per capita in the national accounts.

Figure 3B.10 illustrates this adjustment with data from the United States. The probability density function is plotted on a logarithmic scale, so that the upper tail of the distribution is clearly visible. The light gray curve shows the distribution of household disposable income in the LIS data, after adjusting for underreporting of self-employment income (the distribution is smoothed using Kernel density estimation). The distribution is approximately log normal.

The dark gray curve in figure 3B.10 shows the adjusted distribution with a Pareto tail spliced from $42,600 onward in order to increase the mean of the distribution from $25,126 to $36,334—the national accounts measure of HFCE per capita. The point is chosen to yield a smooth and continuous transition from the survey distribution to the Pareto tail (which explains why the transition is not visible in the figure). Because the population captured by the unadjusted and adjusted bell curves (given by the area under each curve) must be the same, a thicker upper tail in the adjusted curve requires a reduction in the density in the lower part of the distribution. The adjusted distribution includes fewer people at lower income levels and more people at high income levels, increasing the mean of the distribution up to the level of HFCE per capita.[22]

---

22. This adjustment essentially involves solving a set of three simultaneous equations with three unknowns. The three constraints/equations are as follows: (a) The distribution is continuous, so that the probability density function of the Kernel density and the Pareto distribution are equal at the splice point; (b) the distribution is smooth, so that the slope of the two distributions at the splice point is the same; and (c) the mean of the joint distribu-

Figure 3B.9 Impact of adjustment on ratio of mean income in household surveys to national accounts measure of household final consumption expenditure per capita

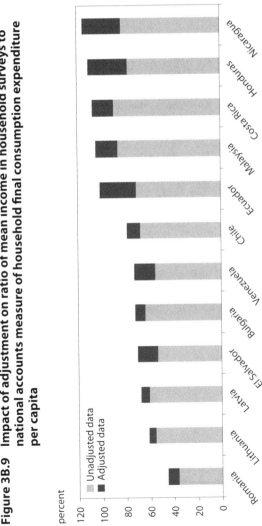

Note: The figure is based on the most recent data available for each country. It includes countries reporting income in the non-LIS sample. The y-axis shows survey mean as percent of household final consumption expenditure per capita.
Sources: World Bank's PovcalNet database for household survey data on incomes; World Bank national accounts data for household final consumption expenditure.

Figure 3B.10 Estimated income distribution in the United States before and after adjustment for undersampling of rich households, 2015

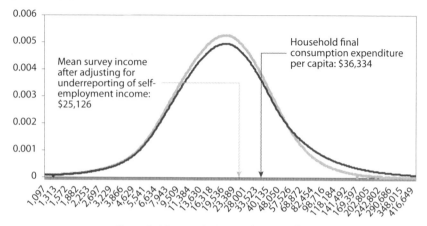

percent of population

annual household per capita income (2011 purchasing power parity dollars)

······ Data adjusted for underreporting of self-employment income

—— Data adjusted for underreporting of self-employment income and undersampling of rich households

Note: Data are adjusted for underreporting of self-employment income.

Sources: Luxembourg Income Study for household survey data on disposable income; World Bank national accounts data for household final consumption expenditure.

In five countries (Denmark, Korea, Norway, the Netherlands, and Paraguay), the adjustment for underreporting of self-employment income brings the mean disposable income in the LIS survey above the HFCE per capita. For these countries, all household disposable incomes are adjusted downward by the factor necessary to render mean income or consumption equal to HFCE per capita, and no further adjustment is applied to the upper tail. This adjustment is sizable only for Paraguay and Korea. In the non-LIS sample, all means that exceed HFCE per capita are adjusted down-

tion is equal to HFCE per capita. The three unknowns are (a) the downward adjustment of the population below the splice point, (b) the position of the splice point, and (c) the Pareto coefficient, which determines how quickly the Pareto tail converges to zero. A similar Pareto adjustment is applied to the non-LIS sample. For these countries the Pareto tail is appended to a log-normal distribution whose parameters are derived from the survey mean and the Gini index provided by the World Bank.

ward to the level of HFCE per capita, keeping the Gini unchanged. For these 28 economies no further Pareto adjustment to the upper tail is applied.[23]

Adjustment Method for China

China requires a unique adjustment method because of its enormous size and exceptionally high household saving rate. If the method applied to other LIS countries were applied to the Chinese data, the adjustment for underreporting of income by the self-employed would result in the adjusted survey mean income exceeding HFCE per capita in the national accounts by 42 percent—close to the household saving rate in China (38.5 percent in 2013, according to the OECD).

Consumption—the variable of interest here—could be captured either by measuring it directly or by deflating the income data to reflect the high saving rate. Fortunately, China is one of the few countries in the LIS that collects detailed microdata on household consumption. These data are available only for urban households, however. Rural consumption is imputed by using rural income data and the relationship between income and the saving rate obtained from the urban sample.

The relationship between the logarithm of income and the household saving rate in the urban sample is reasonably robust, particularly at lower income levels (corresponding to the incomes of much of the rural population).[24] The fitted values from this relationship are used together with the household-level income information for rural households to impute household consumption for rural households. Together with the reported consumption of urban households, these data allow the distribution of consumption in China to be estimated. Mean per capita household consumption calculated using this method amounts to 81 percent of HFCE per capita. The remaining 19 percent of the gap is closed using the Pareto adjustment.

These adjustments have significant effect on measured inequality in China. The Gini index using unadjusted income data from the LIS is 53.3. When consumption data are used instead, it falls to 48.4, because the saving rate rises with income. The Pareto adjustment to the upper tail increases in-

---

23. The economies in this group are Afghanistan, Bolivia, Bosnia and Herzegovina, Burundi, the Central African Republic, the Democratic Republic of the Congo, Ecuador, Ethiopia, the Gambia, Guinea, Hong Kong, Lebanon, Malaysia, Mauritania, New Zealand, Nicaragua, Niger, Papua New Guinea, Portugal, Puerto Rico, Singapore, Swaziland, Tajikistan, Uganda, Vietnam, Yemen, and Zimbabwe.

24. The fact that the average saving rate in urban households in the LIS data (25.0 percent) is significantly lower than the OECD data for China as a whole (38.5 percent) may reflect greater underreporting of income than consumption by survey respondents. It may also reflect undersampling of high-income households, which have higher saving rates.

equality as in other countries. The final adjusted Chinese distribution used in this analysis has a Gini index of 56.3.

Effect of Adjustments on Within-Country Inequality

Pareto adjustment of the upper tail mechanically increases within-country inequality (see figure 3.2). Because of data limitations, the adjustments ignore some of the drivers of the gap between surveys and national accounts. These drivers may be more relevant for some countries than others. In countries with high rates of homeownership, for example, exclusion of imputed rent in surveys leads to a significant downward bias in reported household incomes. Ideally, one would want to correct this bias before making the Pareto adjustment. The method presented here likely overstates inequality in these countries, both in absolute terms and relative to other countries with lower homeownership rates.

Applying the optimal adjustment to each country's data on an individual basis using the most comprehensive information set available is beyond the scope of this analysis. Instead, a simple and transparent method of adjustment was applied consistently across all countries in the sample, using only data available for all countries. This method leads to a situation in which some pairwise comparisons of adjusted Gini indices look implausible (Serbia is almost certainly less unequal than Brazil). Such individual cases notwithstanding, the Gini indices based on adjusted and unadjusted data presented in figure 3.2 are highly correlated (correlation coefficient of 0.9).

Comparison with Previous Studies that Adjust Survey Data

The method used here is inspired by the pioneering approach of Christoph Lakner and Branko Milanović (2013). It expands on that approach in three respects. First, whereas Lakner and Milanović adjust only the upper tail, the method presented here adjusts the survey data for underreporting of self-employment income first. Doing so reduces the size of the gap that needs to be closed using Pareto interpolation as well as the extent of implausibly large shares of income being attributed to the richest households in a number of emerging-market economies with large gaps between surveys and national accounts (notably India). Second, whereas Lakner and Milanović assume that all of the gap represents underreporting, the method presented here allows for both underreporting and sample truncation. Third, whereas Lakner and Milanović apply their adjustment to the top 10 percent of the distribution, the method presented here allows the data to determine where the adjustment is required, consistent with a smooth and continuous distribution.

Sudhir Anand and Paul Segal (2015) employ a somewhat different methodology. They assume that surveys accurately capture the bottom 99 percent of the population but miss the top 1 percent in all countries. They use data on top income shares from the World Top Incomes Database (www.wid.world), which come from tax records, to append the top percentile.

Tax authorities may well capture top incomes much more accurately than household surveys, but there are problems with combining the two data sources, for several reasons. First, tax records measure pretax income, whereas survey measures of inequality are usually based on disposable income (after taxes and transfers), the more relevant measure of living standards. To the extent that pretax income is distributed more unequally than disposable income in countries in which income tax is progressive, these figures likely overstate top disposable income shares.

Second, the unit of analysis differs. Surveys use households, whereas tax records use tax units, which can be individuals or married couples. The tax unit is normally smaller than a household, which may drive a wedge between top income shares using per capita household income and top shares based on tax unit income.

Third, tax records are likely to suffer from their own measurement errors and omissions. For example, tax evasion and avoidance by the rich is likely to bias downward top income shares based on data reported to the tax authorities. In addition, some types of capital income may not be taxed in which case they would not appear in tax records.

The severity of these data issues is likely related to the country's stage of development, which makes it problematic to impute top income shares for the vast majority of emerging-market economies based on the relationship between survey and tax records from mostly advanced economies, as Anand and Segal are forced to do because of data availability constraints. Furthermore, the assumption that the problem of sample truncation is identical across countries (exclusion of the top 1 percent everywhere) is questionable. Capturing the upper tail of the distribution in surveys is likely to be more difficult in some emerging-market economies, where the rich tend to live behind the walls of gated communities, out of reach of survey fieldwork officers.

The approach pioneered by Anand and Segal (2015) is an important complement to the method using national accounts. Each can serve as a robustness check on the other.[25] Appending the Pareto tail to survey data in a smooth and continuous fashion could be done using information

---

25. The estimate of global inequality in Anand and Segal is very similar to that presented in chapter 4. Average figures, of course, hide significant differences in the distribution of individual income groups across countries and regions.

from the World Top Incomes Database in place of national accounts data. Doing so would generate a more flexible framework than that implied by the assumption by Anand and Segal that surveys exclude only the top 1 percent. Such an adjustment is beyond the scope of this analysis.

4

Global Income Distribution from the Turn of the Century to 2035

*As long as poverty, injustice, and gross inequality persist in our world,
none of us can truly rest.*

—Nelson Mandela

Globalization—in trade, media coverage, travel—means that people are now more aware of a wider circle of people than they once were. A consequence is an intensifying interest in global disparities in living standards.

Distributional data from different countries require careful adjustments before they can be pieced together to complete the global puzzle. The picture of global inequality that emerges is closer to an impressionist painting than a photograph. The contours are clear, however, and the key message stark and powerful: Global income inequality is vast, much greater than inequality observed within most countries.

The picture takes on a more hopeful hue when one considers changes in the global distribution over time. Since the turn of the century, rapid economic growth in several emerging-market economies, including some of the world's most populous countries, has helped reduce global inequality. Under current projections as many as half a billion people will emerge from poverty over the next two decades, and global inequality will continue to decline.

How Do Philosophers Think about Global Inequality?

Most philosophical analysis of distributive justice has focused on the distribution of resources and opportunities within countries. Growing awareness of global disparities in living standards has raised new questions that have begun to be addressed. Do people have stronger obligations toward citizens of their own country than they do toward foreigners? If so, how can such stronger obligations be justified?

"Humanitarian" obligations to help people in need and avoid willfully harming others for personal gain are relatively uncontroversial. They are grounded in people's shared humanity, regardless of residence, nationality, ethnicity, religion, or other differences. These obligations hold by virtue of the absolute rather than the relative level of need. They demand an end to absolute poverty in the world rather than a reduction in the disparities in relative living standards or opportunities.

The moral implications of these disparities are more controversial. The growing philosophical literature on global distributive justice has produced eloquent arguments for why people should feel morally outraged by the scale of global inequality—and equally eloquent arguments for why they should be more concerned about inequalities within their own countries. Positions range from wholehearted cosmopolitanism (the notion that one should treat all individuals identically) to denial of any moral responsibility for justice at the international level (see Blake and Smith 2015 and Weisman 2015 for excellent reviews).

Some philosophers argue that the enormous differences in access to resources and opportunities that people face by virtue of their place of birth are difficult to reconcile with reasonable criteria of entitlement (Caney 2005).[1] This view would suggest that people should be just as outraged by gaping disparities in income across the globe as they are about similar disparities within their own countries.

Others believe that distributive equality is relevant only within certain relational contexts. A large body of literature explores the relevance of institutions that structure human interactions and the allocation of the gains from cooperation. John Rawls (1999) distinguishes between the domestic realm and the international realm. In the domestic realm, inequalities in the distribution of goods are acceptable only if they benefit the least well-off people in a society (a concept known as the "difference principle"). In the international realm, the demands of justice are weaker and relate primarily to relationships between states.

Rawls' followers have sought to buttress this distinction by pointing to differences in political structure between the two realms, emphasizing the coercive nature of domestic legal systems. The necessary invasion of individual autonomy by the state requires justification and must reflect the purpose and operation of rules and institutions. Every legal system regulating economic relationships influences the distribution of the benefits of those relationships; the principles that justify them are therefore distribu-

---

1. The premium for living in a rich country is sizable: Using household surveys for more than 100 countries, Branko Milanović (2015) estimates that where people live accounts for more than two-thirds of the variation in their incomes.

tive, describing fair relative shares to which each citizen is entitled. Because no such coercive legal system exists at the international level, the demands of international justice are weaker (Blake 2001, Freeman 2006, Risse 2006). Thomas Nagel (2005) takes this argument further, arguing that the lack of a coercive international legal system undermines all claims of justice outside the state.

Some "institutionalists" have sought to extend the domain of interpersonal distributive justice to the global level by arguing that international institutions are also coercive (Abizadeh 2007, Cohen and Sabel 2009, Cavallero 2010) or by denying the relevance of coercion and arguing that cooperative relationships are sufficient to give rise to principles of distributive justice (Sangiovanni 2007, Moellendorf 2011).

"Communitarians" also emphasize the moral relevance of human relationships, but of a rather different kind. They have been critical of the liberal project of constructing abstract principles of justice that apply universally to the basic institutions of society, arguing that the relationships most important to human flourishing are always specific. Indeed, Michael J. Sandel (2009) argues that it is impossible for humans to behave as though they were "unencumbered selves" under Rawls' "veil of ignorance." People are by nature encumbered by loyalties to family, community, and other groupings defined by religion, culture, or nationality. The norms and traditions of a community can provide the intellectual framework within which people reason about which objectives to pursue in their lives (MacIntyre 1981). The implication of these theories is that nations, cultures, and communities need support and that principles of justice that are sensitive to this need may allow for a preference for the good of one's own community over that of others.

Estimating Global Inequality: Key Concepts and Issues

Most analyses of the global distribution of resources focus on differences in incomes or economic growth either across countries or within countries; few studies put the two together. Cross-country studies examine differences in total or average per capita incomes, economic growth rates, and other macroeconomic measures (see Jones 2015 for a recent review). Within-country studies compare the degree of such inequality across countries or its evolution over time within a country (Hellebrandt 2014, OECD 2015a). Numerous studies explore whether countries with higher within-country inequality experience slower economic growth (Forbes 2000; Ostry, Berg, and Tsangarides 2014).

Efforts to estimate the global distribution of individual incomes have been under way since the late 1990s (see, for example, Chotikapanich,

Valenzuela, and Rao 1997; Schultz 1998; Bhalla 2002; Bourguignon and Morrisson 2002; Milanović 2002, 2005; Dowrick and Akmal 2005; Sala-i-Martín 2006; Lakner and Milanović 2013, 2016; Anand and Segal 2015; and Hellebrandt and Mauro 2015). Branko Milanović (2005) distinguishes three ways of estimating global inequality. "Concept 1" is unweighted international inequality, in which each country is treated as a unit, regardless of the size of its population. Countries are simply lined up from lowest average per capita income to highest and a measure of inequality is computed across these values. "Concept 2" is population-weighted international inequality. The fictional lineup is composed of individuals rather than countries and therefore reflects differences in population. However, it assumes that every person in a country earns the average per capita income, ignoring within-country inequality. "Concept 3" is "true" global income inequality; all individuals worldwide take their position in the fictional lineup based on their own per capita household income.

For measuring global income inequality, the advantage of Concept 2 over Concept 1 is clear: If individuals are to be treated equally regardless of nationality, it makes sense to give each country a weight commensurate with its population. Concept 3 is preferable to Concept 2 because average per capita incomes mask differences in income distribution within countries.

Consider, for example, a world with two countries, A and B, with the same per capita income. Country A has large numbers of both poor and rich people; in country B everyone has the same income. Only Concept 3 would reflect greater inequality within country A.

Concept 3 requires information on within-country distributions. These data are obtained from household surveys, which measure income in some countries and consumption in others. Combining income and consumption survey data is necessary because of data constraints. The resulting global distribution can therefore be thought of as either an income distribution or a consumption distribution; this analysis uses the terms interchangeably.

Before data from different countries can be combined, the values of income/consumption, expressed in national currency at current prices, need to be converted to a common numeraire. This conversion is done using the World Bank purchasing power parity conversion factors for 2015 from the 2011 International Comparison Program. Global interpersonal income comparisons more accurately reflect relative purchasing power across countries when purchasing power parity exchange rates are used. Nontraded goods and services, an important component of consumption baskets, tend to be less expensive in emerging-market economies than in advanced economies. Market exchange rates understate this price difference; purchasing power parity exchange rates adjust for the difference.

The global distribution of income can be estimated by aggregating individual country income/consumption distributions and scaling them to reflect each country's population. Projections can be made by letting individuals' incomes grow in line with the projected growth in their country's per capita real GDP and rescaling country distributions to reflect population growth.

The baseline projections in this analysis assume that within-country inequality remains unchanged; all incomes in a country are therefore assumed to grow in line with average growth. Alternative scenarios explore how potential changes in within-country distributions would affect the future global distribution.

These estimates of global inequality are more accurate than those of previous studies, for three main reasons. First, they are based on new, high-quality microeconomic data on within-country income distributions from the Luxembourg Income Study (LIS). Second, they include adjustments for underreporting of consumption by the self-employed (an important factor in countries with larger informal economies) and nonreporting by the richest households (see chapter 3). Third, they yield a more complete and accurate picture of the global income and consumption distribution by producing figures for narrowly specified income brackets, making it easier to analyze the implications for specific consumption items.[2] These estimates also represent the first effort to project global inequality 20 years from now.

Global Inequality in 2003, 2015, and 2035

The projections show a flatter distribution in 2035 than in 2015, following an earlier flattening since 2003 (figure 4.1). Median per capita income in 2015 was $2,589 (up from $1,531 in 2003), and the mean was $7,711 (up from $5,970 in 2003). To put these estimates in context, the US poverty line in 2015 for a four-person family with two dependent children was $24,036, or $6,009 per capita. Seventy-one percent of the world's population thus had incomes below the official US poverty line in 2015.[3]

---

2. Previous studies (such as Kharas 2010) project the number of people worldwide and in various regions that will enter the middle class (defined in different ways in each study).

3. This figure may be a slight overestimate, for two reasons. First, the US poverty line increases less than proportionately with family size, because of economies of scale in living costs, and it increases less when a child is added to the household than when an adult is added. Low incomes cause people to economize on housing expenses by living in larger households—for example, by sharing their dwellings with extended family members. In addition, households

Figure 4.1 Estimated (2003 and 2015) and projected (2035) distribution of global income

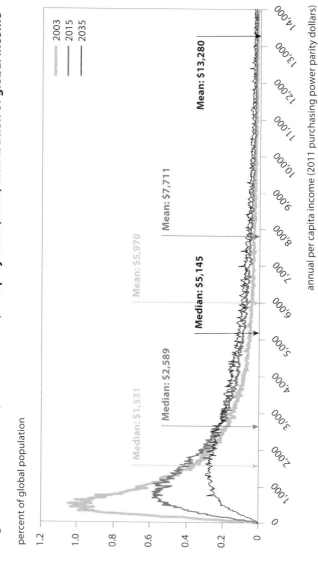

Sources: Luxembourg Income Study and World Bank PovcalNet database for household survey data on income/consumption distribution; World Bank national accounts data for household final consumption expenditure. See appendix 2A for data sources for growth and population projections. See appendices 3B and 4A for methodology.

For the world as a whole, the Gini index was 69.1 in 2015, down from 73.8 in 2003. This figure is much higher than the Gini for the vast majority of countries. The (adjusted) Gini index in the United States, which is high by advanced-economy standards, was 53.7 in 2013 (the date of the latest survey). Most emerging-market economies in the sample of countries for which high-quality and internationally comparable LIS data are available had Gini indices below 65 in recent years.

An alternative inequality measure is the 90:10 ratio, which measures the ratio of the income of people in the 90th percentile of the distribution to that of people in the 10th percentile. For most advanced economies, the results show that this ratio has been below 5 in recent years, meaning that the income of people in the 90th percentile in the domestic distribution is less than five times that of people in the 10th percentile. For the United States, this ratio was 6.8 in 2013. For the world as a whole, the ratio was 28.5 in 2015.

The worldwide median individual income is projected to double, to $5,145 in 2035, and average individual income is projected at $13,280. The global Gini index is projected to decline to 66.6 and the 90:10 ratio to 25.3. The worldwide distribution of income is thus expected to become less unequal, albeit still more unequal than in most countries. The number of people living in poverty (consumption of less than $1.90 a day) is projected to decline from 890 million in 2015 to 400 million in 2035 (box 4.1).

The main driving force behind the shift toward greater equality worldwide is more rapid growth in per capita incomes in emerging-market economies than in advanced economies. Faster population growth rates in some poorer countries, particularly in Sub-Saharan Africa, will constrain the decline in global inequality, however. Indeed, in a hypothetical scenario of zero population growth everywhere in the world, the global Gini index in 2035 would fall from the baseline projection of 66.6 to 65.2.

Christoph Lakner and Milanović (2016) show that global inequality was broadly stable between 1988 and 2003 and began to fall thereafter (figure

in emerging-market economies have more children than in the United States. Thus, a lower per capita poverty threshold would probably be appropriate in many of those countries. Second, if the prices on which purchasing power parity conversion factors are based are sampled disproportionately from urban areas in emerging-market economies (as Chen and Ravallion 2010 claim), the average price level will be biased upward and the incomes of the rural populations understated when expressed in purchasing power parity terms. Lakner and Milanović (2013) attempt to adjust for this factor. Their analysis suggests that the effect of such adjustment on estimates of global inequality is small.

Box 4.1   What would it take to eliminate global poverty?

The poverty headcount (defined as the number of people living on less than $1.90 a day in 2011 purchasing power parity dollars) fell from 2.0 billion in 1990 to 900 million in 2012 (World Bank Group 2016). The analysis in this book (based on different data for some countries and not designed specifically to estimate poverty) puts the number of global poor in 2015 at 890 million. The declining trend is projected to continue over the next 20 years, reaching 400 million poor people (4.7 percent of the global population) by 2035.

If it were possible to impose a tax on the global rich and transfer it costlessly to the global poor, absolute poverty could be eliminated at a stroke. The tax rate would not need to be very high. If it were levied only on the top 1 percent of the global population—people with annual income of at least $67,968 (in purchasing power parity terms)—the rate required to eliminate global poverty in 2015 would have been 1.1 percent of their income. Broadening the tax base to the top 5 percent (people earning at least $26,811), 10 percent (people earning at least $17,034), or 20 percent (people earning at least $9,175) would reduce the tax rate needed to eliminate global poverty significantly (figure 4.1.1). If the tax were levied only on people in these income brackets who live in rich countries, the tax rate would have to be only a little bit higher than if it were levied globally.

Figure 4.1.1   Income tax on the "rich" needed to eliminate global poverty

income tax rate needed to eliminate global poverty (percent)

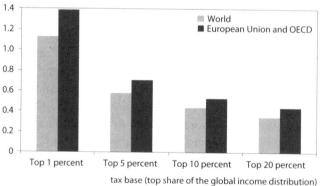

tax base (top share of the global income distribution)

OECD = Organization for Economic Cooperation and Development

Note: Calculations are based on the strong assumption of zero cost of administering the redistribution scheme. Poverty is defined as annual per capita income of less than $694 (in 2011 purchasing power parity dollars), based on the World Bank threshold of $1.90 a day.

Sources: Luxembourg Income Study and World Bank PovcalNet database for household survey data on income/consumption distribution; World Bank national accounts data for household final consumption expenditure.

(box continues)

Actually eliminating global poverty by imposing such a tax would not be easy to do, as Deaton (2015) notes. Most international aid goes to governments, not individuals; for a variety of reasons, too little of it reaches the poorest people. In the absence of reliable citizen identification schemes, means testing (verification that an individual's income is below a certain threshold), and ways of transferring funds to recipients in low-income countries, international aid would have to continue to be channeled through governments, reducing its effectiveness. Nevertheless, the results suggest that the humanitarian obligation to aid fellow human beings in desperate need should not be dismissed out of hand as an idealistic dream that demands too much sacrifice to even contemplate.

4.2).[4] Other studies (Edward and Sumner 2013; Lahoti, Jayadev, and Reddy 2016) corroborate their results. The results presented here confirm this trend and suggest that the decline is likely to persist. It would mark a stark change from trends observed during the past two centuries: François Bourguignon and Christian Morrisson (2002) estimate that global inequality rose significantly and continuously between the early 19th century and 1992 (when their data end).

The rise of China helped reduce global inequality over the past decade. One way to quantify the importance of its contribution is to calculate what the global Gini index in 2015 would have been if the Chinese economy had not taken off. Had per capita income growth in China over the 2003–15 period equaled the average of the rest of the world, the global Gini index would have fallen to 71.2, a decline of a little over half as much as was observed. The projected decline in the rate of Chinese growth and the population explosion forecast in Africa help explain why global inequality is projected to decline more slowly between 2015 and 2035 than it did between 2003 and 2015.

The difference between the global Gini indices obtained here and in Lakner and Milanović (2016) reflects differences in methodology. Lakner and Milanović use survey data only, without any adjustments. The method used here (described in appendix 3B) closes the gap between survey means and household final consumption expenditure in the national accounts by adjusting for underreporting of self-employment income and under-

---

4. The baseline results in Lakner and Milanović (2016) are based on the 2005 round of the World Bank's International Comparison Program. The authors provide a robustness check based on the 2011 round.

Figure 4.2   Three estimates of the global Gini index, 1988–2035

Gini index

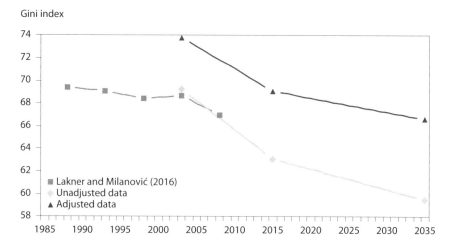

Sources: Luxembourg Income Study and World Bank PovcalNet database for household survey data on income/consumption distribution; World Bank national accounts data for household final consumption expenditure. See appendix 2A for data sources for growth and population projections. See appendices 3B and 4A for methodology.

sampling of rich households. This method yields higher inequality, both within countries and globally.

Regardless of which of the methods illustrated in figure 4.2 is used, global inequality is projected to decline significantly between 2015 and 2035, continuing a trend that began in the early 2000s. The 2.5-point decline between 2015 and 2035 or even the 7.2-point decline between 2003 and 2035 might appear small in the context of the large range of within-country inequalities. However, these declines are sizable compared with the changes in inequality observed within countries in recent decades. Unadjusted data from the LIS reveal that the Gini index in the United States increased from its trough in 1979 to its peak in 2013 by 5.8 Gini points. In the United Kingdom the increase over the 1979–2010 period was 6.6 Gini points. A widespread perception in both countries is that the increases in inequality were large and transformative. The 4.5-point decline in Mexico's Gini over 1998–2010 is associated with perceptions of an improvement in income distribution in that country. Reducing inequality in the United States by 7.2 Gini points would require an annual transfer of about $3,700 from every person in the top half of the US income distribution (households with per capita incomes above $18,600) to every person in the bottom half. The projected decline in global inequality over 2003–35 in the baseline scenario may thus be considered sizable.

Table 4.1 Contributions of between-country, within-country, and overlap components to global inequality, 2003 and 2015

Item	2003	2015	Change
Total Gini index	73.8	69.1	−4.7
Between-country component	57.4	48.2	−9.2
Within-country component	2.3	3.0	0.6
Overlap component	14.0	17.9	3.8

Sources: Luxembourg Income Study and World Bank PovcalNet database for household survey data on income/consumption distribution; World Bank national accounts data for household final consumption expenditure. See appendix 2A for data sources for growth and population projections. See appendices 3B and 4A for methodology.

What Drives Changes in Global Inequality?

Table 4.1 decomposes the Gini index into three components. The "within" component is the weighted sum of all within-country inequalities, with the weights given by the product of a country's share in world population and its share in world income. The "between" component is the weighted sum of the relative distance between each pair of countries' mean incomes. It roughly corresponds to Concept 2 inequality described above. The "overlap" component is the residual, which captures the fact that the income distributions of different countries overlap (so that some people living in relatively poor countries are better off than some people living in relatively rich countries) (see Milanović 2005 for details on the methodology).

The "between" component is the driver of the decline in the Gini index between 2003 and 2015 (table 4.1). Within-country inequality in fact increased a little, on a weighted average basis. Convergence in average national living standards has thus been far more significant in reducing global inequality over the past decade than changes in income distributions within countries.

The relatively large overlap component stems primarily from the convergence in mean incomes over this period. More rapid growth in emerging-market economies than in advanced economies increased the share of the population in the former group that approached (and in some cases surpassed) advanced-economy standards of living; the degree of overlap between countries' distributions therefore increased. Income growth for relatively rich people living in relatively poor countries mitigates the equalizing effect on the global distribution of convergence in average standards of living.

The importance of the overlap between countries' distributions illustrates the importance of using individual-level data. Using only country means would ignore not only the relatively small effect of changes in within-country inequality but also the much larger effect from the overlap between countries' distributions, which is significant even when within-country inequality remains constant. Ignoring the overlap would lead to overestimating the decline in global inequality between 2003 and 2015.

The overlap component also explains why the reduction in global inequality over the recent past and the projection period is somewhat smaller when the survey data are adjusted in the ways described in appendix 3B. Compared with the unadjusted survey data, the adjustments increase the thickness of the upper tail of within-country income distributions and thus increase the number of relatively rich people living in relatively poor countries.

Geographic Distribution of World Population by Income

As the number of people at different income levels grows at different rates in countries and regions over the next 20 years, the regional makeup of the global distribution will change. By 2035 the bottom decile will be even more heavily concentrated in Sub-Saharan Africa, which will account for almost 70 percent of that group, up from 50 percent in 2015 (figure 4.3). Many emerging-market economies, particularly China and India, will account for larger shares of the top decile. China's share of this group will increase from 6 percent in 2015 to 15 percent in 2035. In contrast, the share of economies classified as advanced will fall from 72 percent to 56 percent in the top decile, continuing a trend that emerged over the past decade (Anand and Segal 2016).

People's consumption choices are determined by how much they earn (absolute incomes) rather than how their earnings compare with other people's earnings (relative incomes). Figure 4.4 shows the regional composition of the global income distribution in 2015 and 2035 with absolute incomes rather than income deciles on the x-axis. The growth of the global economy can be seen in the rightward shift of the global distribution toward higher incomes, with the areas indicating emerging-market economies generally shifting further than the area indicating advanced economies.

The global income distribution can be broken down into broad income brackets that correspond roughly to the consumption of particular types of goods, as discussed in chapter 5. In 2015, 3 billion people had annual incomes of less than $2,000, and just 560 million had incomes of $20,000 or more (figure 4.5). As the global population and average per capita incomes rise, more and more people will find themselves in higher income brackets. The number of people in the lowest income bracket is projected to decline by more than 1.1 billion by 2035, despite population growth

Figure 4.3   Estimated (2015) and projected (2035) regional composition of global income, by income decile

a. 2015

percent of global income for the decile

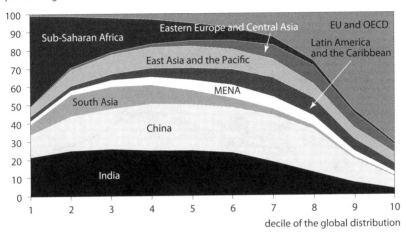

decile of the global distribution

b. 2035

percent of global income for the decile

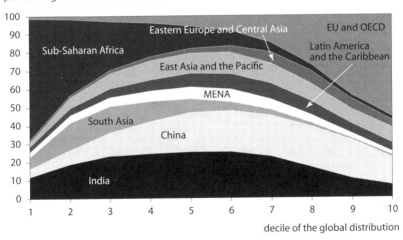

decile of the global distribution

OECD = Organization for Economic Cooperation and Development; MENA = Middle East and North Africa

Note: Projections are based on the baseline assumptions. The y-axis reports the shares accounted for by each region/country in total global income for each decile (noted on the x-axis) of the global distribution.

Sources: Luxembourg Income Study and World Bank PovcalNet database for household survey data on income/consumption distribution; World Bank national accounts data for household final consumption expenditure. See appendix 2A for data sources for growth and population projections. See appendices 3B and 4A for methodology.

Figure 4.4   Estimated (2015) and projected (2035) regional composition of global income distribution

a. 2015

percent of global population

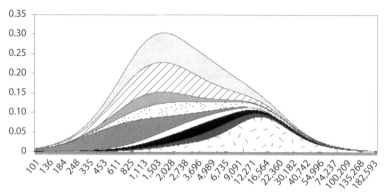

annual per capita income (2011 purchasing power parity dollars)

b. 2035

percent of global population

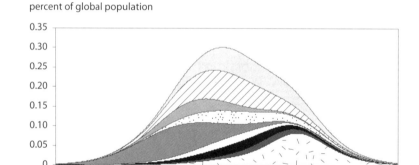

annual per capita income (2011 purchasing power parity dollars)

European Union and OECD   Eastern Europe and Central Asia
Latin America and the Caribbean   Middle East and North Africa
Sub-Saharan Africa   East Asia and the Pacific
South Asia   India   China

OECD = Organization for Economic Cooperation and Development

Note: Income is reported on a logarithmic scale on the horizontal axis to make the upper tail visible. Projections are based on baseline assumptions.

Sources: Luxembourg Income Study and World Bank PovcalNet database for household survey data on income/consumption distribution; World Bank national accounts data for household final consumption expenditure. See appendix 2A for data sources for growth and population projections. See appendices 3B and 4A for methodology.

Figure 4.5   Estimated (2015) and projected (2035) world population, by region and income bracket

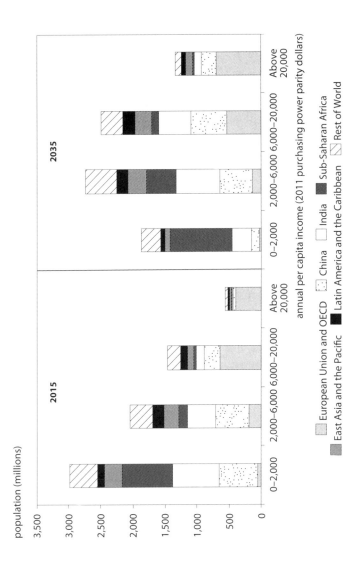

population (millions)

annual per capita income (2011 purchasing power parity dollars)

European Union and OECD   China   India   Sub-Saharan Africa

East Asia and the Pacific   Latin America and the Caribbean   Rest of World

OECD = Organization for Economic Cooperation and Development

Note: Projections are based on the baseline assumptions.

Sources: Luxembourg Income Study and World Bank PovcalNet database for household survey data on income/consumption distribution; World Bank national accounts data for household final consumption expenditure. See appendix 2A for data sources for growth and population projections. See appendices 3B and 4A for methodology.

and its concentration in Sub-Saharan Africa. The number of people with per capita incomes of $2,000–$6,000 will increase by 690 million, with the largest gains in Sub-Saharan Africa and India. Most of the population growth in Sub-Saharan Africa will be concentrated in this bracket over the next 20 years. The number of people with incomes of $6,000–$20,000 will increase by a little over a billion, with the largest gains in India and China. The number of people earning more than $20,000 a year will increase by 780 million, with the largest gains in the advanced economies and China.

Sensitivity of Projections of Global Inequality

What If Within-Country Inequality Increases?

The projected decline in global inequality depends in part on the assumption that within-country inequality remains unchanged. A significant rise in inequality within countries would offset some of the effect of differential growth rates between advanced and emerging-market economies and thus moderate the projected decline in global inequality. For worldwide inequality to remain unchanged over the next two decades, within-country inequality would have to increase by 6.2 Gini points.[5]

A country's Gini index might well rise by 6.2 points (Indonesia's index rose from 29.3 in 1987 to 35.6 in 2010, for example, an increase of 6.3 points). A uniform increase of this magnitude across all countries would be unprecedented, however. Among the 15 largest countries by population for which there is sufficient data coverage over a roughly 20-year period, only two (Indonesia and China) experienced an increase of more than 5 Gini points between the late 1980s/early 1990s and 2010. Four (Brazil, Russia, Iran, and Thailand) saw decreases of more than 5 points; the remainder saw changes in the plus or minus 5-point range.[6]

The population-weighted average increase in within-country inequality (based on unadjusted survey data) for all countries for which data were available amounted to 1.5 points over the past 15–20 years. Over the past 10 years or so, there was almost no change. It thus seems very unlikely that increases in within-country inequality would be large enough to offset the impact of cross-country differences in economic growth.

---

5. This calculation assumes that inequality rises uniformly in all countries. It is based on a log-normal distribution of incomes for all countries in the sample, including countries for which microdata are available from the LIS (the Gini indices and country means remain unchanged). The simplifying assumption of log normality in the LIS sample has only a minor impact on the estimate of global inequality.

6. See appendix 3A for data sources.

This required offsetting increase in within-country inequality is greater than the projected fall in global inequality (2.5 Gini points) because of the complex relationship between global and within-country inequality. To see why, consider a world made up of two countries (say, India and the United States). India is projected to grow faster than the United States; this catch-up growth will mechanically reduce global inequality. What is the effect on global inequality of rising inequality within both countries? Relatively rich Americans would see their incomes grow faster than average, pulling away from the global mean and increasing global inequality. But relatively poor Americans would be brought closer to the global mean, which would reduce global inequality. The converse would be true in India: Rapid income growth of relatively rich Indians would reduce global inequality, but relatively slow income growth of poor Indians would raise global inequality. Because of these partially offsetting effects in each country, within-country inequality would have to rise by more than the projected fall in global inequality in order to fully offset it.

What If Within-Country Inequality Evolves According to the Kuznets Hypothesis?

Within-country inequality could evolve during the next 20 years in accordance with the estimated cross-country Kuznets curve (see chapter 3). This scenario implies that economic growth is accompanied by rising inequality in the poorest countries of the world but that once a country reaches a certain level of development further growth is associated with falling inequality. If the Kuznets curve relationship estimated in figure 3.3 continued to hold over the next 20 years, some of the most populous countries in the world would see a significant decline in inequality. Under this scenario, the Gini index would decline from 56.3 in 2015 to 45.0 in 2035 in China and from 55.7 to 51.0 in India.[7] The global Gini index would fall more than twice as fast in this alternative scenario, from 69.1 in 2015 to 63.0 in 2035 (compared with 66.6 in the baseline scenario).

---

7. The projected decline in inequality in China under the Kuznets scenario is the largest in the world (as chapter 3 shows). China is now located close to the peak of the estimated Kuznets curve, and its consumption is projected to grow rapidly (5.7 percent a year on average), implying that it would make significant progress along the downward-sloping part of the curve. If the Kuznets curve is not stable over time, as suggested by time-series evidence, the projected decline would be attenuated.

Figure 4.6   Effect on global inequality of greater than projected growth in six countries

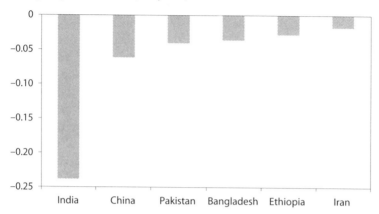

change in global Gini index (Gini points)

Note: The figure shows the effect on inequality if each country's economy in 2035 were 10 percent larger than under the baseline. The length of the bar indicates how much smaller the global Gini index would be in 2035 than in the baseline scenario.

Sources: Luxembourg Income Study and World Bank PovcalNet database for household survey data on income/consumption distribution; World Bank national accounts data for household final consumption expenditure. See appendix 2A for data sources for growth and population projections. See appendices 3B and 4A for methodology.

What If Certain Countries or Regions Grow More Rapidly than under the Baseline?

The magnitude of the projected decline in global inequality depends on the speed with which emerging-market economies converge toward advanced-economy income levels. Forecasting these changes is difficult; individual countries could perform better or worse than the baseline projections.

Which countries and regions matter most in this regard? Figure 4.6 shows the top six countries in terms of the effect on the global Gini index if their economies were 10 percent larger in 2035 than assumed in the baseline projection.[8] This assumption increases the average annual growth rate of household consumption by 0.45 percentage points. India has by far the biggest effect, because it is projected to be the world's most populous country in 2035 and because it is expected to remain relatively poor. China's population is projected to be only 11 percent lower than India's in 2035, but per capita household consumption is expected to be 63 percent higher. Indeed,

---

8. The effect is broadly, though not exactly, symmetric if the economy in question is 10 percent smaller in 2035 than assumed in the baseline.

Figure 4.7 Effect on global inequality of greater than projected growth in six regions

change in global Gini index (Gini points)

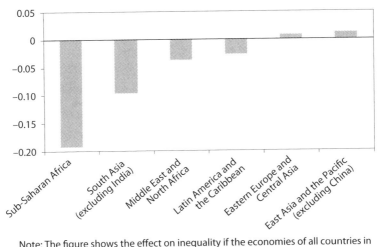

Note: The figure shows the effect on inequality if the economies of all countries in the region were 10 percent larger in 2035 than under the baseline. The length of the bars indicates how much smaller (or larger) the global Gini index would be in 2035 than in the baseline scenario.

Sources: Luxembourg Income Study and World Bank PovcalNet database for household survey data on income/consumption distribution; World Bank national accounts data for household final consumption expenditure. See appendix 2A for data sources for growth and population projections. See appendices 3B and 4A for methodology.

mean household consumption in China is projected to be only slightly below the global mean. Additional growth in China would therefore have a much smaller effect on global inequality than additional growth in India.

Figure 4.7 shows the effect on the global Gini if all countries in a region were 10 percent larger in 2035 than assumed in the baseline scenario. Sub-Saharan Africa is the region whose growth is most important in influencing the evolution of global inequality. Growth in East Asia (excluding China) that is faster than projected in the baseline scenario would raise global inequality, because the baseline projections already assume that mean income in East Asia will significantly surpass the global mean by 2035 (by 9 percent).

An optimistic scenario assumes that income and consumption in four of the most populous emerging-market economies—China, India, Indonesia, and Nigeria, home to a projected 3.6 billion people in 2035—grow 0.5 standard deviations faster than the baseline and that all other countries grow at the baseline rate. This faster rate of convergence would result in a steeper decline in the global Gini index, to 66.1 in 2035. Under this scenario, the global poverty rate would fall to 4.3 percent (360 million people).

What If Growth Reverts to the Mean?

Under the more pessimistic, reversion to the mean scenario, each country's growth rate is assumed to gradually revert to the worldwide sample mean observed during the past 50 years (see chapter 2 for details). As emerging-market economies are growing more rapidly than advanced economies on average, the downward revision in growth projections is larger in the former than in the latter. This scenario yields a smaller reduction in global inequality (a Gini index of 68.2 in 2035). The number of people below the World Bank poverty threshold of $1.90 a day would decline to 670 million (7.9 percent of the sample population) in 2035, compared with 400 million (4.7 percent) under the baseline scenario. The shifts into middle- and higher-income groups would also be more muted. In the event of the even more pessimistic scenario for Africa discussed in chapter 2 (in which there is no further convergence of African economies toward more advanced economies after 2015), global inequality would fall even less (a Gini index of 68.4 in 2035), and the global poverty rate would fall only to 8.6 percent.

Benefits of Using Individual-Level Data

One of the key claims made in this book is that using individual-level data leads to more accurate estimates and projections than relying exclusively on aggregate macro-level data such as GDP per capita. Its validity can be shown by comparing Concept 2 and Concept 3 inequality, as defined by Milanović (2005) and discussed at the beginning of this chapter. Concept 3 inequality is based on individual-level information obtained from household surveys. It assigns to each resident in a country his or her actual income or consumption. Concept 2 inequality ignores the within-country distribution of incomes and instead assigns to each resident the countrywide average per capita income or consumption. Concept 2 leads to significantly lower estimates of global inequality than Concept 3, because it ignores within-country inequality (table 4.2).

There is also a significant effect on the estimated change in global inequality. Under all scenarios, Concept 2 leads to a greater decline in inequality than Concept 3. The difference reflects the overlap between income distributions in different countries, which Concept 2 ignores. In the preferred method (Concept 3), which takes into consideration the significant numbers of high-income individuals living in relatively poor countries, growth in their incomes and consumption dampens the effect on global inequality of convergence of average standards of living (Milanović 2005).

Table 4.2 Global inequality under different scenarios, 2015 and 2035

	Gini index		
Scenario	2015	2035	Change
Baseline			
Concept 2 (no within-country information)	48.2	40.7	−7.5
Concept 3 (individual-level information)	69.1	66.6	−2.5
Reversion to the mean			
Concept 2 (no within-country information)	48.2	45.1	−3.2
Concept 3 (individual-level information)	69.1	68.2	−0.9
Optimistic			
Concept 2 (no within-country information)	48.2	38.9	−9.4
Concept 3 (individual-level information)	69.1	66.1	−3.0

Sources: Luxembourg Income Study and World Bank PovcalNet database for household survey data on income/consumption distribution; World Bank national accounts data for household final consumption expenditure. See appendix 2A for data sources for growth and population projections. See appendices 3B and 4A for methodology.

Taking Stock and Next Steps in the Analysis

The results reported in this chapter show that global inequality is likely to decline in the next 20 years, but the vast gaps between the rich and the poor will persist. The sensitivity analysis has explored the factors—economic growth in the emerging-market and advanced economies, changes in within-country inequality—that will determine the extent of that decline. The projected global income distribution serves as a stepping stone for an analysis of changes in consumption—the focus of the next chapter.

Appendix 4A Creating a Global Distribution from Within-Country Distributions

The gap between mean income (or consumption) as measured in household surveys and national account aggregates such as per capita household final consumption expenditure (HFCE) raises problems for estimates of global inequality, which are made by combining individual country distributions. Which measure of mean income (or consumption) should be used?

Angus Deaton's (2005, 10) analysis leads him to conclude that "there can be no general presumption in favor of one or other of the surveys and the national accounts." But researchers estimating the distribution of living standards across the world are forced to make a choice, and the choice is of great importance for estimating global inequality. Until recently, two methods were used:

- Method 1: Ignore the discrepancy with the national accounts, and use only unadjusted survey data (see, for example, Hellebrandt and Mauro 2015, Lakner and Milanović 2013, Milanović 2005).

- Method 2: Use distributional information from the survey, and combine it with the mean from the national accounts. In practice this means that all incomes in a survey are scaled up uniformly so that the gap between the survey mean and national accounts is eliminated (for example, if the survey mean is 80 percent of HFCE per capita, then all incomes in the survey are multiplied by a factor of 1.25; inequality remains unchanged but the mean increases by 25 percent). (See, for example, Chotikapanich, Valenzuela, and Rao 1997; Schultz 1998; Dowrick and Akmal 2005; Sala-i-Martín 2006.)

Method 1 is preferable to Method 2. As Sudhir Anand and Paul Segal (2008, 69) note, "given that we take within-country distributions from surveys, it seems anomalous that we should seek an alternative source for the means of these distributions." However, household surveys suffer from measurement problems that bias survey estimates of both mean income and income inequality downward (see appendix 3B). These errors appear to be related to the gap between survey means and HFCE per capita in the national accounts. It would therefore seem appropriate not to ignore the information from national accounts but rather to use it to adjust both the mean and the within-country distributions obtained from survey data.

The preferred method used in this analysis (Method 3, outlined in detail in appendix 3B) adjusts the survey data for underreporting of self-employment income and undersampling of rich households. It closes the gap between surveys and HFCE per capita and increases within-country

Figure 4A.1   Estimated global income distribution using three alternative methods, 2015

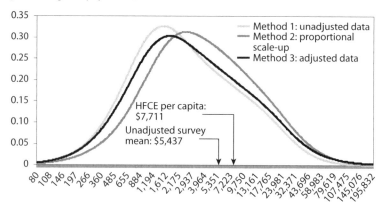

percent of global population

HFCE = household final consumption expenditure

Note: The Method 1 curve (light gray line) shows the distribution of household income based on information from household surveys only. The Method 2 curve (dark gray line) shows the distribution using survey data scaled up proportionately to close the gap between survey mean and HFCE per capita. The Method 3 curve (black line) shows the distribution using data adjusted for underreporting of self-employment income and the Pareto adjustment of the upper tail of within-country distributions. The distributions have been smoothed using Kernel Density estimation.

Sources: Luxembourg Income Study and World Bank PovcalNet database for household survey data on income/consumption distribution; World Bank national accounts data for household final consumption expenditure. See appendix 2A for data sources for growth and population projections. See appendices 3B and 4A for methodology.

inequality. The more comprehensive definition of HFCE in the national accounts seems more appropriate for assessing global disparities in living standards than the survey definition of income or consumption, because items captured in HFCE but missing in surveys (such as housing services, financial intermediation services, and consumption of nonprofit institutions serving households) are likely to contribute (directly or indirectly) to households' well-being.

Figure 4A.1 compares the global income distributions generated by the three methods, plotting income on a logarithmic scale. The light gray line shows the global distribution generated using unadjusted survey data (Method 1). Using this method, the global mean income in 2015 is estimated at $5,437 and the global Gini index is 63.1. The dark gray line shows the results of proportional scaling up of survey incomes to close the gap between survey mean and HFCE per capita in each country (Method 2).

The estimated global mean rises to $7,711 (the global HFCE per capita), but the Gini index falls significantly, to 61.4. The reason for this fall is that the gap between surveys and national accounts is generally larger in poorer countries than in rich ones. The scaling up of incomes to close the gap is therefore larger in poorer countries, reducing between-country inequality while leaving within-country inequality unchanged. The result is an unambiguous decline in estimated global inequality.

The distribution generated by the preferred method is shown in the black line in figure 4A.1 (Method 3). The mean is equal to the global HFCE per capita value of $7,711 but, with a global Gini index of 69.1, the distribution is now more unequal than the one based on unadjusted data. Increasing the thickness of the upper tail of within-country distributions increases the within-country component of global inequality, which more than offsets the reduction in between-country inequality generated by using national account means in place of survey means.

5

How Will Changes in Population and Income Distribution Affect Global Consumption?

> *The poorer is a family, the greater is the proportion of the total [expenditure] which must be used for food....The proportion of the [expenditure] used for food, other things being equal, is the best measure of the material standard of living of a population.*
>
> —Ernst Engel

This chapter examines the impact of rising individual incomes on people's spending choices, by analyzing previous studies and presenting new estimates based on household survey data for 20 economies and 7 consumption categories (food and beverages, transportation, clothing and apparel, housing and equipment, education, health, and other). It then combines these estimates with projections of the global income distribution (reported in chapter 4) to project global consumption for each category. Detailed results are provided for food and beverages (henceforth referred to as "food") and transportation—the two categories whose shares in total consumption are found to be significantly affected by rising incomes. Chapter 6 examines the implications of the projected changes in consumption for investment in infrastructure.

Because household surveys do not provide income or consumption data by age group, the analysis does not estimate the impact of projected changes in the population's age structure on consumption choices. It also ignores the impact of consumer demand on prices. The analysis should therefore be viewed as complementary to other efforts to project private consumption and infrastructure needs, which relax some of these assumptions.[1]

---

1. Earlier projections—of spending on transportation (OECD and ITF 2015), energy consumption (IEA 2015), and infrastructure requirements (OECD 2012), for example—use a combination of bottom-up and top-down approaches or multiequation models. Some of these models project demand for various transportation modes (road, rail, ship, air, freight, passenger). These estimates generally do not use the distribution of household incomes within individual

How Do Rising Incomes Affect Individual Economic Choices?

Economists have long studied how changes in a person's income affect his or her economic behavior, with emphasis on the types of goods and services chosen. In the 19th century, German economist Ernst Engel (1857, 1895) showed that household expenditures on food rise with income and family size but that the share of food in a household's budgets decreases with income. This relationship, known as Engel's law, is one of the most robust relationships in economics.[2]

Constructing "Engel curves" is the first step in projecting global demand for various goods and services. Researchers can do so using data from household surveys or macroeconomic data.

Household-level information provides more accurate projections, for three reasons. First, it permits a more precise analysis of the relationship between total consumption and the share of consumption allocated to a given spending category, because the number of observations far exceeds the number from cross-country comparisons. Second, unlike country averages, household surveys contain information on consumption choices by individuals with relatively low or relatively high incomes. Third, the relationship between a household's consumption and the share of consumption it allocates to particular types of goods is not always linear; the increase depends on an individual's income at the beginning of the period. Forecasts of the growth of, say, transportation consumption in a given country therefore depend not only on forecasted changes in the country's average per capita consumption but also on how income gains are distributed.

To illustrate the powerful impact of individual's spending power on consumer choices, figure 5.1 reports the share of India's population at various levels of total household per capita expenditure who owns a bicycle, a scooter, or a car. As income and consumption rise, people get rid of their bicycles and buy scooters; after their annual expenditure reaches about $2,500, they start buying cars.

People begin purchasing certain consumption goods once they reach various income thresholds. The projections of the number of people whose incomes will exceed those thresholds in 20 years (reported in chapter 4) may thus be interpreted as projections of the number of people who will be able to afford the items listed in table 5.1.

---

countries, however; the assumed relationships between income and spending on specific items are based on cross-country relationships estimated using per capita averages. Moreover, studies usually focus on just one or a few expenditure items rather than on total consumption and its subcomponents.

2. The share of spending on food generally declines linearly with the logarithm of income, although there is evidence of nonlinearity at very high and very low incomes (see Lewbel 2006 for references).

Figure 5.1 Ownership of bicycles, scooters, and cars in India, by level of total household per capita expenditure

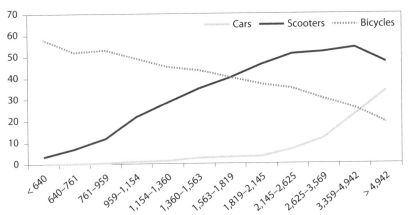

percent of households

annual per capita expenditure (2011 purchasing power parity dollars)

Source: Household Consumption of Various Goods and Services in India 2011–12, National Sample Survey 68th round, Ministry of Statistics and Programme Implementation, Government of India, 2014.

Table 5.1 Consumption patterns for different income brackets (international US dollars)

Annual per capita income	Description	Goods and services purchased
Less than $2,000	Poverty or near-poverty	Basic goods, bicycle
$2,000–$6,000	Entering consumer class	Refrigerator, scooter, cellphone, water purifier, tobacco, more meat and fish, sugary drinks, beer
$6,000–$20,000	Emerging middle class	Car, laptop, washing machine, skin care products, dining out, wine, chocolate
More than $20,000	Global middle class	Retail banking services, air travel

Sources: Chamon, Mauro, and Okawa (2008); Dobbs et al. (2012); Airbus (2015).

As incomes rise, not only do people consume more, they also often shift their spending toward goods that put pressure on natural resources. For example, as their incomes rise, nonvegetarians increase their consumption of meat and fish more than proportionately. These increases contribute to water shortages, overfishing, and climate change.[3]

---

3. Consumption of meat—particularly beef—contributes to emissions of methane, a greenhouse gas that has a more deleterious effect on the climate than carbon dioxide (Foley 2014, Kunzig 2014).

Box 5.1   Impact of rising incomes on consumption of "bads"

Consumption of sugary drinks rises rapidly after people can afford a minimally adequate caloric intake; its share in total consumption declines at higher levels of income. Excess consumption of sugared drinks contributes to obesity and rising costs of health care. Cross-country scatter plots of soda consumption versus GDP per capita show a positive and significant correlation, though outliers (such as the United States and Mexico on the positive side and several Asian countries on the negative side) suggest that cultural and other factors are at play (Credit Suisse 2013).

Consumption of alcoholic drinks tends to rise with incomes, beginning as soon as individuals (more often, men) begin to leave extreme poverty. (As a result, beer companies have been among the earliest and most successful manufacturers in many emerging-market economies.) The share of spending on alcohol in total consumption first rises with income, then declines after incomes reach a certain level.

But there are important exceptions to the generally positive association between income and alcohol consumption for people in the middle of the income distribution. The most prominent example was the tragic increase in mortality among Russian men in the aftermath of the collapse of the Soviet Union. Although additional factors may have been at play, it seems that as these men saw their incomes and social structure crumble, they turned to consumption of cheaper and more harmful forms of liquor (Brainerd and Cutler 2005). Similar factors—job losses as well as stagnant or declining incomes and relative status—help explain rising death rates for middle-age white non-Hispanic men in the United States during the past two decades. Drug and alcohol poisoning, suicide, and chronic liver diseases account for the increase (Case and Deaton 2015).

Smoking (of at least one cigarette a day) is prevalent in some of the poorest countries on earth, even among some of the lowest-income groups.[1] The poor may even use smoking as an appetite suppressant. One of us once reluctantly agreed to ride in a cycle rickshaw in Indonesia. At noon the rickshaw driver paused for a moment, lit a cigarette, and explained "lunch." In contrast, in rich countries smoking is less prevalent among high-income groups; education and peer effects may be driving the relationship (Pampel 2010).

---

1. Data are available from the World Health Organization's Global Health Data Repository, http://apps.who.int/gho/data/node.main.65.

For some items, people do not necessarily increase consumption when income rises. This is especially evident for tobacco products or for types of food or drink for which it is difficult to draw the line between "goods" and "bads," such as alcohol and sugared drinks. In such cases, the link with income is often obscured by variation in education, personal sense of self-worth, and stress (box 5.1).

The impact of rising incomes is beginning to be investigated for many important life choices beyond consumption. For example, in developing economies higher incomes increase the likelihood that people migrate. According to research summarized by Michael A. Clemens (2014), throughout the late 20th century the relationship between emigration and real income per capita had an inverted *U*-shape, whose curvature became more pronounced over time: In the per capita income range between $600 (that of Niger or Ethiopia today) and $7,500 (Albania or Colombia today), countries with higher per capita incomes experienced more emigration. By the end of the 20th century, richer countries in this range on average had nine percentage points more migration abroad than the poorest countries in the same range.[4] For countries with per capita incomes above $7,500, the relationship is reversed. The evidence thus suggests that when people are very poor, rising incomes are more likely to lead them to emigrate but that after they reach middle-income levels further income gains make them less prone to leave their country of origin.

A possible interpretation of this finding is that people living in extreme poverty lack both information on and the means to migrate. In a telling example from fiction, Lila and Lena, 12-year olds in the 1950s Neapolitan impoverished neighborhood depicted by Elena Ferrante in *My Brilliant Friend*, have never seen the sea—even though their city hugs the Mediterranean.

A back-of-the-envelope calculation based on the individual income projections presented in chapter 4 suggests that the number of people earning $2,000–8,000—who would seem most interested in migrating across national borders, based on Clemens' (2014) review—is likely to double over the next 20 years, with the largest increases in Sub-Saharan Africa, South Asia, and India. This doubling of the potential pool of migrants suggests that, other things equal, actual migration across national borders is likely to rise significantly from current levels. The extent of the actual increase will depend on a host of factors including conflicts, climate change, and restrictions by recipient countries.

New Estimates of Impact of Rising Incomes on Spending Choices

The estimates presented here focus on how rising incomes affect individuals' shares of spending on seven categories (food and beverages, transportation, clothing and apparel, housing and equipment, education, health,

---

4. These results would overturn conventional wisdom about the effectiveness of aid to low-income economies as a means of stemming migration flows (Clemens 2014).

and other), using data from household surveys for 20 economies.[5] This is the first estimation of Engel curves for those categories for a sample of several advanced and emerging-market economies.

The share of spending on each category is regressed on the natural logarithm of total consumption (in 2011 purchasing power parity dollars).[6] For each survey, average consumption of each category is calculated for households in each total individual consumption range. Total consumption ranges are defined by narrow, $100 increments (yielding, for example, the $10,000–$10,100 range), to enhance the precision of the estimates. Each of these averages constitutes a data point for estimating the relationship between per capita household consumption and spending on each category of goods and services.

Figure 5.2 shows the negative, broadly linear relationship between the logarithm of total individual consumption and the share of spending on food. The relationship is estimated by pooling all data points for all countries in the sample.[7] The results are consistent with Engel's law.[8]

Figure 5.3 reveals a positive, more nonlinear empirical association between the logarithm of total individual consumption and the share of spending on transportation in the same economies. The relationship is convex at lower income levels (the share of spending rises more steeply

---

5. The estimates include only direct spending by consumers. Food does not include government subsidies. Transportation covers only transit by people, not the transport of goods. The data come from three sources. Data for Albania (2008), Bangladesh (2010), Brazil (2008), Colombia (2010), Indonesia (2010), India (2011), Mexico (2010), Malawi (2010), Pakistan (2010), South Africa (2010), Uganda (2009), and Vietnam (2008) are from the World Bank's Global Consumption Database. Data for Australia (2010), France (2010), Hungary (2012), Mexico (2010), Poland (2010), Russia (2013), Slovenia (2010), South Africa (2010), and Taiwan (2010 are from the LIS. Data for the United States (2013) are from the Consumption Expenditure Survey (conducted by the Bureau of Labor Statistics). Each survey covers several thousand individuals. Data on Mexico and South Africa come from two surveys. They yield slightly different shares spent on food and transportation at each individual income level, but the patterns are similar. Both the Global Consumption Database and the LIS seek to ensure cross-country comparability of the surveys, including the definition of spending categories.

6. The use of logarithms, which is customary in studies of this kind, makes it more likely that some of the relationships—notably between total consumption and the share of food in total consumption—will be linear.

7. The results are similar if the estimated curves for each country are allowed to have their own intercepts, to reflect any country-specific factors that may influence average consumption of specific categories. (Such factors include any remaining differences in the way the surveys define the categories, despite efforts to make the surveys internationally comparable.) The slope and curvature are estimated under the assumption that they are the same in all countries.

8. More detailed estimates (not reported) show that the share of beverages (especially alcohol and sugary drinks) in total consumption declines more slowly than the share of food. The share of meat and fish in total consumption also declines more slowly than the share of food generally.

Figure 5.2 Estimated Engel curves for food based on household survey data from 20 economies

percent of income spent on food

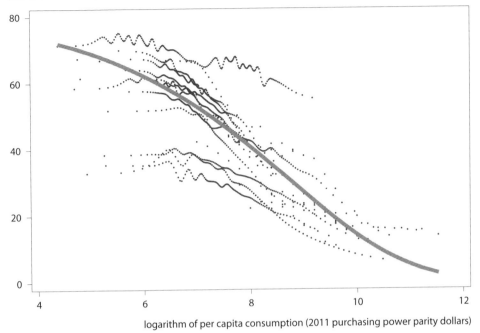

logarithm of per capita consumption (2011 purchasing power parity dollars)

Note: The figure was estimated using a logistic function based on panel data. "Food" includes both food and beverages.
Sources: Data from the World Bank Global Consumption Database, the Luxembourg Income Study, and the Consumer Expenditure Survey (conducted by the US Bureau of Labor Statistics).

as income grows). It becomes concave at higher income levels (the share of spending rises less steeply as satiation sets in). The fitted relationships in figures 5.2 and 5.3 are estimated using functions (logistic for food and Gompertz for transportation) that allow for the possibility of an S-shape, if warranted by the data.[9]

9. Both the logistic and the Gompertz function have the potential for two asymptotes (instances in which the relationship becomes flatter and flatter and eventually horizontal), one at very low incomes and the other at very high income levels. The logistic form is symmetric, whereas the Gompertz can be asymmetric. The choice between them was based on goodness of fit and consistency with previous analyses on related topics. For food the logistic function is preferred to the Gompertz function, because it provides slightly better fit and the estimated coefficients imply that although very-high-income individuals reduce their share of food in overall consumption, they continue to increase the absolute amount of expenditure on food as incomes rise. For transportation a Gompertz function is estimated, as in several studies of the market for cars (for example, Dargay, Gately, and Sommer 2007,

Figure 5.3 Estimated Engel curves for transportation based on household survey data from 20 economies

percent of income spent on transportation

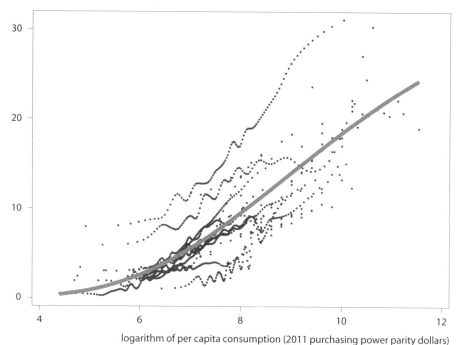

logarithm of per capita consumption (2011 purchasing power parity dollars)

Note: The figure was estimated using a Gompertz function based on panel data.
Sources: Data from the World Bank Global Consumption Database, the Luxembourg Income Study, and the Consumer Expenditure Survey (conducted by the US Bureau of Labor Statistics).

The estimated Engel curves for both food and transportation display strong goodness of fit (adjusted R^2 of 0.95 for food and 0.86 for transportation). As in many previous studies, the estimated slope for food is negative and linear for most income levels. At very high income levels, the relationship flattens, becoming nearly horizontal. Table 5.2 shows the estimated coefficients, based on 1,293 observations (each of which is an average of many household-level observations within a narrowly defined range of individual consumption).

The share of transportation spending in total consumption is flat at low levels of total consumption, rises as consumption increases to levels typically associated with advanced economies, and then becomes flatter. The *S*-

who estimate a Gompertz function relating average per capita real incomes and the average number of cars in the population for a cross section of countries).

Table 5.2 Estimated Engel curve coefficients for food and transportation based on household survey data

Coefficient	Estimate	Standard error
Food		
b_1	72.70	2.53
b_2	−0.77	0.05
b_3	8.29	0.10
Transportation		
b_1	36.55	4.90
b_2	0.34	0.04
b_3	8.86	0.41

Note: The coefficients for food are based on the logistic model $\frac{F}{C} = \frac{b_1}{1 + e^{[-b_2(\ln C - b_3)]}}$. The coefficients for transportation are based on the Gompertz model $\frac{T}{C} = b_1 e^{\{-e^{[-b_2(\ln C - b_3)]}\}}$.

shape for total transportation spending is less pronounced (less nonlinear) than in studies of cars alone (Dargay, Gately, and Sommer 2007; Chamon, Mauro, and Okawa 2008), perhaps as a result of two factors. First, households are not able to afford cars when their incomes are below a minimum threshold (estimated by Chamon, Mauro, and Okawa at $5,000 a year based on a panel of countries). Second, in several advanced economies, satiation is observed for car travel at high income levels; it is less likely to affect spending on transportation more generally, including air travel.[10]

The shares of food and transportation in total spending change significantly as individual incomes rise. People whose total annual consumption is $200 a year spend an estimated 66.3 percent of their total consumption on food and 1.2 percent on transportation. When total consumption reaches $200,000 a year, the figure for food falls to 3.4 percent and the figure for transportation rises to 26.4 percent (table 5.3).

The estimated spending share is also reported for the remaining categories (clothing and apparel, housing and equipment, education, health, and other), based on the corresponding Engel curves (linear).[11] In contrast to the estimates for food and transportation, estimates for these categories

---

10. Passenger vehicle travel declined in recent years in several advanced economies, notably Japan and the United Kingdom (OECD and ITF 2015).

11. Estimation of the Engel curve for health allows for different intercepts for each country, to reduce the influence of the United States, an outlier with much higher healthcare spending at all income levels.

Table 5.3   Estimated consumption shares of various categories of goods and services at different levels of total annual consumption (shares in percent of total consumption)

Category	$200	$2,000	$20,000	$200,000
Food	66.3	45.9	16.4	3.4
Housing and equipment	13.4	18.8	24.1	29.4
Clothing and apparel	5.0	5.1	5.1	5.2
Health	2.9	3.6	4.3	5.0
Education	1.6	2.8	3.9	5.1
Transportation	1.2	7.9	18.0	26.4
Other (residual)	9.5	16.0	28.1	25.5
Other (regression-based)	6.5	16.1	25.5	35.0

Note: "Other (residual)" is the difference between 100 percent and the sum of the shares of all other categories. "Other (regression-based)" is from the estimated Engel curve for the category "other" in the data.

Source: Data from the World Bank's Global Consumption Database, the Luxembourg Income Study, and the Consumer Expenditure Survey (conducted by the US Bureau of Labor Statistics).

are not robust to changes in the sample or the estimation technique and are therefore not pursued further.[12]

Projected Spending on Food and Transportation

This section combines two sets of data to project demand for food and transportation by 2035. The first is projections of total consumption at the individual level worldwide, obtained in chapter 4 by combining the individual distribution of incomes (or consumption) within each country in 2015 with projections for each country's GDP growth between 2015 and 2035. The second is the Engel curves displayed in the previous section. Each individual worldwide is assigned the amount of each consumption category that can be read off the Engel curves at his or her income level. Summing the consumption of each category over all individuals yields category totals for each country and for the world as a whole.

---

12. The share of health care in total spending bears no clear relationship to individual incomes, in contrast to the strong positive association between the share of healthcare spending and average GDP per capita documented in studies based on time-series information from macroeconomic data (see, for example, Jones 2015). The absence of an empirical association in the microeconomic data casts doubt on the notion that health is a luxury good (i.e., a good whose demand rises more than proportionally with income), pointing instead to increases in the relative cost of health care over time as a key driving factor.

Figure 5.4   Projected cumulative growth in total consumption, transportation, and food between 2015 and 2035, by country and region

projected cumulative growth (percent)

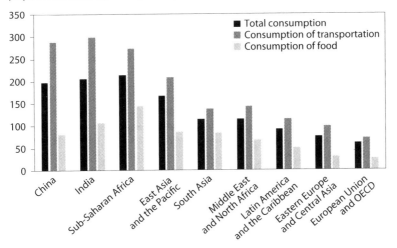

Note: Data are in constant prices.

Sources: Data from the World Bank Global Consumption Database, the Luxembourg Income Study, and the Consumer Expenditure Survey (conducted by the US Bureau of Labor Statistics).

Figure 5.4 reports the projected growth rates (in constant prices) between 2015 and 2035 for food and transportation by country or region. Spending on transportation is projected to increase by 300 percent in India, 290 percent in China, 275 percent in Sub-Saharan Africa, 210 percent in East Asia and the Pacific, and 100–150 percent in all remaining emerging-market regions. The increase is projected to be smallest (70 percent) in the European Union (EU)/Organization for Economic Cooperation and Development (OECD) group.

Using the full within-country distribution of individual incomes is valuable, because many individuals are in sections of the Engel curve that are flatter than in the vicinity of average per capita consumption. Had country averages of total per capita consumption been used in conjunction with the micro-based Engel curves reported in figures 5.2 and 5.3, the projected growth rates of transportation consumption would have been considerably higher for all countries and regions—by as much as 60–70 percentage points in India and Sub-Saharan Africa—primarily because the mean individual income in a country's or region's total consumption distribution is usually in the steepest section of the transportation Engel curve.

For food consumption, the highest growth rate is projected for Sub-Saharan Africa (145 percent), stemming in part from the rapid growth of total consumption there (the gap between the growth rates of food consumption and total consumption is relatively small, because of the sizable initial share of food in total consumption).[13] Total spending on food increases by 110 percent in India and 80–90 percent in East Asia and the Pacific, South Asia, and China. The lowest growth rates for food spending (25–30 percent) are projected for the European Union/OECD, Eastern Europe, and Central Asia.

The global share of food is projected to decline to 14.8 percent of total consumption in 2035, down from 18.7 percent in 2015 (table 5.4). The average transportation share in total consumption is projected to rise to 20.1 percent, up from 18.3 percent in 2015. Shifts in consumption patterns vary widely across countries or regions, with larger increases in the transportation share in emerging-market economies.

Table 5.4 also reports the cumulative increase in food and transportation between 2015 and 2035, expressed as a share of 2015 consumption. Higher increases in transportation spending as a share of the initial size of the economy suggest a greater challenge to finance the supporting infrastructure investment. The largest increases are projected for transportation in China (49.9 percent), India (43.6 percent), and Sub-Saharan Africa (42.8 percent).

Total consumption and transportation spending will increase more in emerging-market economies than advanced economies over the next 20 years (figure 5.5). Despite slower projected economic growth in the advanced economies, however, they will continue to account for a sizable share of the global increase in both total and transportation spending. Annual consumption of transportation services will increase at an annual rate of 4.2 percent globally and 5.8 percent in non-OECD economies between 2015 and 2035.[14] In emerging-market economies, the transportation sector will account for more than a quarter of the increase in total consumption in the next two decades.

Increases in consumption of both transportation and food will raise greenhouse gas emissions and put pressure on natural resources. In the emerging-market economies in particular, the heavier weight of transporta-

---

13. The gap between the growth rates of spending on food (F) and overall consumption (C) equals $\frac{dF/F}{dC/C} = \left[1 + \frac{C}{F}\frac{d(F/C)}{d(\ln C)}\right]$. It thus depends not only on the slope of the Engel curve $\left(\frac{d(F/C)}{d(\ln C)}\right)$ but also (negatively) on the initial ratio of spending category F to total consumption.

14. These projections are higher than some others. The OECD and ITF (2015) estimate that road and rail passenger travel will grow at an annual rate of 2.3–3.5 percent globally and 3.6–5.0 percent in non-OECD economies through 2050.

Table 5.4   Estimated (2015) and projected (2035) spending on food and transportation, by region or country

Country or region	Cumulative increase as percent of total initial consumption		Food share (percent of total consumption)		Transportation share (percent of total consumption)	
	Food	Transportation	2015	2035	2015	2035
Countries						
China	22.2	41.5	27.4	16.7	14.5	18.8
India	33.6	38.7	31.5	21.3	13.0	16.9
Regions						
East Asia and the Pacific	18.0	37.0	20.7	14.5	17.7	20.5
Eastern Europe and Central Asia	6.0	17.0	20.5	15.2	17.2	19.5
European Union and OECD	3.4	15.0	12.8	10.1	20.8	22.3
Latin America and the Caribbean	10.6	19.4	21.4	16.7	17.0	19.0
Middle East and North Africa	15.2	24.4	22.4	17.5	17.2	19.4
South Asia	24.7	20.0	29.6	25.3	14.5	16.0
Sub-Saharan Africa	42.3	41.1	29.3	22.8	15.0	17.9
World	11.9	23.3	18.7	14.8	18.3	20.1

OECD = Organization for Economic Cooperation and Development
Source: Data from the World Bank's Global Consumption Database.

Figure 5.5   Projected rise in spending on transportation and nontransportation, 2015–35

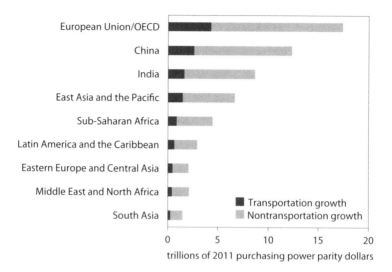

trillions of 2011 purchasing power parity dollars

OECD = Organization for Economic Cooperation and Development

Sources: Data from the World Bank Global Consumption Database, the Luxembourg Income Study, and the Consumer Expenditure Survey (conducted by the US Bureau of Labor Statistics).

tion in the total consumption increase suggests a rise in the relative importance of this sector in future greenhouse gas emissions.[15] Increased food consumption will also have serious environmental effects. Consumption of meat and fish rise with income. They require more energy and water to produce and yield more carbon dioxide emissions than vegetarian sources of calories and protein. Deforestation, desertification, and overfishing may also ensue, unless measures are taken to keep them in check. Policymakers will need to take these effects into account as they plan for the future.

---

15. The share of carbon dioxide emissions attributable to transportation in the largest emerging-market economies was less than 10 percent before 2012 (IEA 2015).

6

Projected Demand for Transportation Infrastructure through 2035

Rapid growth in consumption—especially transportation services—will require massive investment in roads, railways, airports, and energy plants. Advanced economies will need to maintain or upgrade their existing infrastructure. Many emerging-market economies will need to build vast new networks to reach a broader share of their populations. This chapter provides tentative estimates of the scale of the new road and railway networks required.

Projections of infrastructure needs have followed four complementary paths:

- Aggregation of projections from experts in specific infrastructure areas (airports, harbors, railways, metros, roads) (OECD 2012).

- Surveys of thousands of executives in more than 100 countries (World Economic Forum 2015).

- Extrapolation of past trends (Dobbs et al. 2013).

- Regression of actual infrastructure provision against physical/geographic characteristics, demographic factors, and economic variables.

Each of these approaches has strengths and weaknesses. Bottom-up estimates (the first two approaches) incorporate the views of experts, but they often lack transparency, because the methods used to project each component may be difficult to retrace or reflect aspirational bias. The perceptions-based approach captures executives' perceptions, but it is subjective. Moreover, it focuses on current rather than prospective needs; it may therefore fail to capture the impact of a rapidly growing population. The top-down approaches (the third and fourth approaches) are transparent and objective, because they rely solely on rules of thumb or regressions, but they do not incorporate technical expert projections or the views of entrepreneurs familiar with the reality on the ground.

The first, third, and fourth approaches are positive rather than normative: They are based on actual choices made by countries in response to various economic factors but are silent on whether such choices meet needs. They also fail to take into consideration the quality of the infrastructure built and whether it provides economic value to society.

Most projections of infrastructure are based on macroeconomic data; only a few consider the distribution of income within countries. One that does (a forecast of demand for air passenger travel) uses the number of households with per capita incomes above a threshold of $20,000 a year (Airbus 2015).

Projecting Demand for Paved Roads and Railroads Based on Past Patterns

This chapter projects demand for paved roads and railroads. It does not examine other important components of infrastructure, such as electricity generation and distribution, for two reasons. The first is data availability. The second is that paved roads and railroads are more closely connected to domestic consumption of goods and services—a key theme of this book—than other types of infrastructure.

The analysis uses information on the distribution of income within countries to improve the goodness of fit of previous studies. It estimates regressions of the length of the paved road and rail networks for a cross-section of countries (76 for railways and 59 for roads), using variables previous studies have found to be significant (the logarithm of real GDP per capita, the logarithm of total population, the logarithm of total land area, and the share of the population living in urban areas) as well as the shares of individuals above income thresholds selected through iterative search for best fit.[1] Inclusion of these thresholds is motivated by evidence of income

---

1. The share of individuals above a given income threshold is from the results of the previous chapters. The data on paved roads are from the International Road Federation (2015). All other data are from the World Bank's *World Development Indicators*. Island city economies (Hong Kong and Singapore in the sample) are outliers (especially with respect to land area and urbanization) and are thus omitted from the estimation. In an effort to improve cross-country comparability, the data on paved roads in India were corrected by excluding paved rural roads built using water-bound macadam (which involves surfacing the roads with a mixture of ground stones, dust, and water) and all rural roads built under the Jawahar Rozgar Yojana public works program (data from Basic Road Statistics of India, 2012, Ministry of Road Transport and Highways, Government of India).

Table 6.1   Cross-country regression results on determinants of length of paved road and railway networks

Variable	Ln(kilometers of paved roads)	Ln(kilometers of railways)
Ln(GDP per capita)	0.664*** (5.55)	0.261* (2.31)
Share of population with annual per capita income of $2,660 in 2014	2.224*** (3.82)	1.797*** (3.67)
Log(population)	0.861*** (10.87)	0.538*** (8.02)
Log(land area)	0.160* (2.20)	0.289*** (4.45)
Urban population (percent)	−3.095*** (−4.43)	−1.105 (−1.70)
Constant	−11.05*** (−10.73)	−7.204*** (−7.03)
R^2	0.911	0.808
Number of observations	59	76

Note: * statistically significant at the 5 percent level. ** statistically significant at the 1 percent level. *** statistically significant at the 0.1 percent level. *t*-statistics in parentheses.

Sources: Data from International Road Federation (2015) and World Bank, *World Development Indicators*.

threshold effects in the demand for cars (Chamon, Mauro, and Okawa 2008). Demand for infrastructure is thus projected based on past empirical associations. Because past spending likely reflects what was possible given budgetary constraints rather than actual needs, it is reasonable to interpret the projections for 2035 as a lower bound.

The results confirm that, other things equal, richer, more populous, larger, and less urbanized countries have more extensive networks of paved roads. The share of population with incomes above $2,660 (the threshold found to best fit the data) is also significantly associated with more extensive networks.[2] The length of the railroad network is significantly correlated with the same variables, except for urbanization.

The projected lengths of the paved road and railroad networks are obtained by applying the coefficients reported in table 6.1 to the projections for GDP per capita and population, the share of the population with incomes above $2,660 in 2035, and projected urbanization rates for 2035 (from the United Nations) for each country. These calculations project that

---

2. The best goodness of fit is found at an income threshold of $2,660 for paved roads and $2,800 for railroads. Given how close the two figures are, a threshold of $2,660 is used in both estimations.

the total length of paved roads will increase by 82 percent, from 20.2 million kilometers in 2014 to 36.8 million kilometers in 2035. Over the same period, the length of the railway network will increase by 44 percent, from 1.1 million kilometers to 1.6 million kilometers (figure 6.1). (These projections are for the countries in the sample, which account for more than 95 percent of world population and output.)

The greatest need for new transportation infrastructure will be in India—the country where the number of people who will be able to afford their first car is growing most rapidly. This finding is particularly striking given that India's paved road network is already more extensive than predicted by cross-country observed patterns (even after omitting rural roads paved with low-quality macadam materials). Other countries/regions where projections suggest the need for rapid growth rates include East Asia, China, and Sub-Saharan Africa.

Inclusion of the $2,660 threshold increases the projections for both types of infrastructure considerably: When the same cross-country regressions are estimated omitting the threshold variable, the projected growth rate of the paved road or rail networks is one quarter to one third lower, and the model's goodness of fit (measured by the adjusted R^2) declines.

These estimates are much higher than others. The International Energy Agency (IEA) projects that the world will need to add nearly 25 million paved-road-lane kilometers and 335,000 rail track kilometers—a 60 percent increase over the combined rail and road network between 2010 and 2050 (over a four-decade rather than a two-decade projection horizon) (Dulac 2013). It projects a doubling of global passenger and freight travel between 2010 and 2050, with non-OECD economies accounting for 90 percent of the increase; passenger travel (which more closely corresponds to consumption of transportation) is projected to account for 70 percent of the increase. The IEA projects cumulative expenditures on transportation infrastructure investment at $45 trillion.[3]

Are the massive increases projected here and by the IEA possible? China tripled its annual passenger and freight travel between 2000 and 2010 and increased its total road and rail network length by 290 percent over the same period (Dulac 2013), suggesting that a sustained boost to infrastructure investment is feasible if sufficient resources are mustered.

A back-of-the-envelope exercise provides a rough indication of the cost of these projects. Assuming (as in Dulac 2013) a per-kilometer cost of $2.6

---

3. Using rule-of-thumb macroeconomic approaches, Dobbs et al. (2013) estimate the cumulative global infrastructure investment need at $57 trillion to $67 trillion over 2013–30. Their estimate includes not only roads and rail but also power, ports, airports, water, and telecommunications.

Figure 6.1 Projected increases in paved road and railroad networks between 2014 and 2035, by region

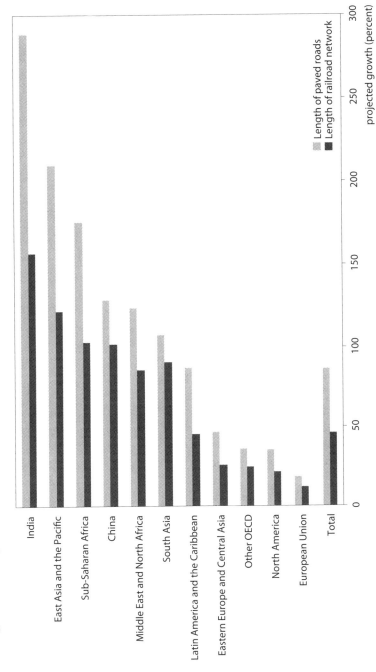

OECD = Organization for Economic Cooperation and Development
Sources: Data from International Road Federation (2015) and World Bank, *World Development Indicators.*

million for paved roads (assumed to have two lanes on average) and $4.5 million for railroads, the cumulative overall cost of building the new infrastructure is $45.5 trillion for paved roads and $2.1 trillion for railroads (these figures do not include operations and maintenance costs). Such investment would cost about 1.3 percent of worldwide GDP a year.

Financing Investment in Infrastructure and Ensuring Value for Money

Do historical patterns suggest that governments will increase investment spending to accommodate rising needs for more infrastructure? The few studies on this topic find little evidence of a link between infrastructure needs and actual spending. Santiago Acosta-Ormaechea and Atsuyoshi Morozumi (2013) analyze the correlation between the share of government expenditure on various items and per capita GDP for a cross section of countries. They find no significant relationship between per capita GDP and government spending on transportation or infrastructure in general. William Easterly and Sergio Rebelo (1993) find that, although public investment on transportation is correlated with economic growth, the share of transportation in total public expenditure bears a small but statistically significant negative correlation with GDP per capita. A possible interpretation of these findings is that scarce budgetary resources have constrained investment in transportation infrastructure, despite its potential benefits for economic growth.

Even if governments are able to muster sufficient resources for investment, additional spending will result in high-quality infrastructure only if measures are in place to prevent the siphoning off of funds by corrupt bureaucrats. Infrastructure investment is especially prone to corruption. A study by the Organization for Economic Cooperation and Development (OECD 2014) reports that almost 60 percent of foreign bribery cases occurred in sectors related to infrastructure and that a large share of corruption cases involves officials of state-owned enterprises. Another study (OECD 2016) documents cases in which engineers, contractors, and public officials colluded to allocate contracts, rig procurement bidding processes, engage in false invoicing, extract illicit payments, illegally finance political parties, and use shoddy workmanship and substandard materials; in some cases, buildings collapsed and people were killed as a result. Benjamin Olken (2007) documents corruption related to road-building projects in Indonesia. The IMF (2015) finds that the quality of the institutions that plan and implement public investment has a significant impact on the efficiency and productivity of infrastructure investment.

Figure 6.2 Estimated correlation between Control of Corruption Index and measure of projected transportation spending

increase in transportation spending

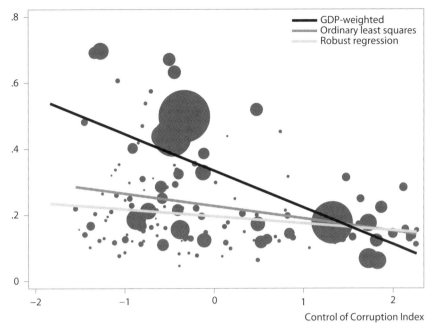

Control of Corruption Index

Note: The y-axis shows the cumulative increase in spending on transportation in 2014–35 divided by total consumption in 2014. The x-axis shows the World Bank's Control of Corruption Index; the higher the index, the lower the level of corruption. The size of the bubbles represents projected GDP in 2035. An automated procedure that reduces the influence of outliers was used to generate the robust regression fitted lines.
Sources: Data from the World Bank's *Worldwide Governance Indicators* (2015 update) and estimates from chapter 5.

Many of the countries with the greatest need for additional infrastructure investment in the next 20 years have weak institutions for selecting and implementing investment projects. The World Bank's control of corruption index is a proxy for the quality of such institutions. The relationship between this measure and the need for additional infrastructure in transportation is negative—that is, countries that will need to spend more tend to have less control over corruption than countries that will need to spend less. The correlation is –0.27 for the projected increase in transportation spending (figure 6.2) and –0.40 for the projected increase in paved roads (figure 6.3), both statistically significant at the 1 percent level.

Figure 6.3 Estimated correlation between Control of Corruption Index and projected increase in paved roads

percent increase in paved roads

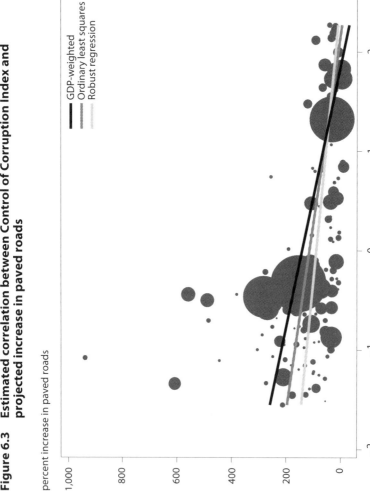

Note: The higher the index, the lower the level of corruption. The size of the bubbles represents projected GDP in 2035. An automated procedure that reduces the influence of outliers was used to generate the robust regression fitted lines.

Sources: Data from the World Bank's *Worldwide Governance Indicators* (2015 update) and estimates from chapter 5.

7

How Will Countries Build the Infrastructure They Need?

If you build it, [they] will come.
—*Field of Dreams*, 1989

Publicity is justly commended as a remedy for social and industrial diseases. Sunlight is said to be the best of disinfectants; electric light the most efficient policeman.
—Justice Louis D. Brandeis

Emerging-market economies will need to construct trillions of dollars worth of new roads and railways in the next two decades, as hundreds of millions of their people join the modern consumer classes. New infrastructure can foster economic growth and accommodate consumer demand. It can also help reduce inequality—by allowing people in rural areas to participate in modern economic activity, for example. This chapter examines how countries can finance this investment and what governments and international bodies can do to reduce the risk of corruption or waste and enhance financial incentives for choosing climate-friendly infrastructure.

Should Policymakers Make a Big Push for Infrastructure Investment?

In the movie *Field of Dreams*, the protagonist (played by Kevin Costner) hears voices telling him that if he builds a baseball field, the sport's past heroes will return from the dead to play there. In the magic of the movies, the heroes oblige, to the protagonist's and spectators' delight. If massive new transportation networks are built in the next 20 years, will demand be sufficient to justify their cost?

The projected increase in spending on transportation (chapter 5) and associated infrastructure needs (chapter 6) suggests that a boost to infrastructure will easily be met by rising demand. Nevertheless, the extent and modalities of desirable involvement by national governments or international institutions in fostering additional investment in infrastructure deserve in-depth analysis.

129

The case for boosting investment in infrastructure through direct public investment as well as policies to facilitate private sector involvement is stronger when infrastructure has a large causal impact on economic growth and the market fails to generate sufficient profit incentives for private providers to close the shortfall in supply. Some studies find that infrastructure investment fosters economic growth. In many advanced economies, including the United States, the initial buildup of transportation networks spurred rapid economic growth. Canals and railways were key to economic development in the 19th and early 20th centuries (Fogel 1964). The interstate highway system contributed to a large one-time productivity boost in the United States in the 1950s and 1960s. John G. Fernald (1999) shows that such investment in roads was associated with a more than proportional increase in industries for which roads are more important, though the benefits diminished as networks were extended in later decades.

Several features of infrastructure investment also argue in favor of government involvement. Projects tend to be large, take years to complete, and involve considerable uncertainty—all considerations that make them risky for private investors. In addition, the benefits of infrastructure projects accrue not only to their users but also to the economy more generally, through increased market size and greater demand for a wide range of goods and services. These considerations formed the rationale for the "big push" model first proposed by economist Paul N. Rosenstein-Rodan (1943) to promote reconstruction and economic development after World War II (box 7.1). Counterbalancing these considerations are concerns about possible corruption and waste in government projects.

In most countries, government involvement goes well beyond setting and enforcing the rules of the game to include direct financing and management of individual projects. The scale of the private sector's involvement depends on country-specific circumstances, including the government's ability to provide a hospitable business environment and the relative abilities of the government and the private sector to access financing.

Creating Room in Fiscal Policies for Public Financing of Infrastructure Investment

To invigorate directly financed infrastructure investment, governments can collect additional revenues, reduce other spending, or increase the fiscal deficit. Previous analyses of how countries' tax and spending choices evolved in past decades have shown that the rise in the revenue-to-GDP ratio as per capita incomes increase has generally been gradual. Based on that historical experience, it seems unlikely that revenue hikes alone would be sufficient to meet global public investment needs through 2035. Moreover,

Box 7.1   Is the time right for a new "big push"?

During the 1940s–1960s, a model known as the "big push" was popular. The concept—first proposed by economist Paul Rosenstein-Rodan (1943) (and expanded upon by Murphy, Shleifer, and Vishny 1989)—argues that building (or rebuilding) underdeveloped areas requires simultaneous investment in many sectors, because development of one sector improves the well-being of workers and entrepreneurs, increasing demand for the goods of other sectors, expanding their market size and making it easier to exploit economies of scale. No sector can break even developing alone, but simultaneous development of many sectors of the economy can be profitable for both individual sectors and the economy as a whole. Coordination can thus move the economy from a bad equilibrium to a good one.

Rosenstein-Rodan wrote during World War II. Given the difficulties businesses would have encountered securing international financing after the war, he proposed the creation of an "East European Investment Trust," financed through grants and loans by governments. His proposal was not a call for a state-controlled economy but rather a plan for the kind of massive infrastructure investment financed by the United States under the Marshall Plan or by the World Bank in the 1950s and 1960s.

Not all economists agree that a big push to infrastructure investment by governments is appropriate or needed to jumpstart economic development. According to Fishlow (1965), railroads in the United States generally made money before the Civil War; investment from the national or state governments was therefore not necessary (see Majevski 2006). To the extent it occurred at all, government investment led to "excess and wasteful construction," according to Fishlow. Railroads produced a high social rate of returns only in the context of a vibrant market economy. He warned that developing economies, especially economies with "frequently wasteful government intervention," should avoid mechanistically investing in "social overhead capital."

Warner (2014) documents a contemporaneous correlation between capital spending and output growth, which he attributes to the effect of spending on output (Keynesian demand effects). But he also finds that public investment drives have often been followed by lower economic growth. (He notes the exception of Ethiopia, where state-controlled public investment led to a significant acceleration of economic growth during the past decade.) Moreover, he reports that many large infrastructure projects funded by the World Bank in the 1970s seem to have had weak outcomes.

competing priorities (including health care, pensions, education, and defense) have often constrained reallocation of expenditure toward investment in infrastructure (Easterly and Rebelo 1993, Acosta-Ormaechea and Morozumi 2013).

Governments that decide to use public funds to revitalize infrastructure must determine how to finance it. Countries with fiscal rules such as deficit caps may consider modifying the rule to exclude public investment from the calculation of expenditures. (Public investment spending would still be subject to parliamentary approval and recorded in the fiscal accounts.) An argument often used to support this approach is that the benefits of public investment continue long after the spending occurs.

There are two arguments against modifying fiscal rules in this manner to permit higher public investment without breaching the deficit caps. First, other spending categories, such as health care and education, can also be viewed as valuable investments for the future and may be less prone to leakage of funds as a result of corruption than infrastructure.[1] Second, excluding public investment infrastructure from the calculation of government expenditures has often led to reclassification of current expenditure items as infrastructure. Taking these considerations into account, excluding infrastructure from deficit caps is more likely to be beneficial in countries with high-quality institutions.

Perhaps as a result, only a small share of fiscal rules adopted around the world has excluded infrastructure investment. The most notable is the United Kingdom's "golden rule," in place between 1998 and 2008, which stipulated that, over the economic cycle, the government should borrow only to invest.[2]

For countries with large public debts (as a share of GDP) or projected debt payments (as a share of exports or fiscal revenues), the bar for taking on additional debt to finance infrastructure projects should be set relatively high. Infrastructure projects can often increase the growth rate of the economy enough to more than pay for themselves within a few years (IMF 2014)—but only if the projects are well chosen, soundly implemented, and provide value for money. These assumptions are less likely to hold the more projects are under way. An increase in spending on infrastructure investment is desirable and will likely take place in many emerging-market economies. To reduce the risk of debt crisis, it would be wise to finance it in large part by reducing other expenditures or increasing tax revenues—preferably by broadening the tax base.

In view of the multiyear obligations stemming from infrastructure projects, national or subnational governments that scale up public investment should adopt medium-term budgetary frameworks or expenditure ceilings that provide multiyear projections. Doing so helps safeguard in-

---

1. One of us (Mauro 1998) finds that higher corruption is associated with lower spending on health care and education. The complexity and unique design features of individual infrastructure projects often make them difficult to price and thus prone to corruption.

2. Borrowing to finance current expenditures was permitted during recessions, but surpluses were required during economic booms to compensate.

frastructure projects from interruptions before completion or payment arrears that might stem from lack of funds or shifting priorities. It is also good practice for projections and ceilings to be subject to parliamentary approval, in order to increase transparency and provide checks on the executive branch's design and implementation of fiscal policy.

Facilitating Private Sector Financing of Infrastructure Projects

Even if fiscal policies are revisited to create more room for government-financed infrastructure, the necessary scale of infrastructure buildup in the next 20 years will likely exceed governments' ability to finance it on their own. At the same time, the long gestation of infrastructure projects implies that the risks are too great for the private sector to bear without guarantees from the government. Cooperation will therefore be critical, particularly in projects that build new infrastructure ("greenfield" projects), which are risker than projects that maintain, renovate, or expand existing infrastructure ("brownfield" projects).

Private sector financing of infrastructure projects takes many forms, only some of which are discussed here (see OECD 2015b for a more comprehensive and detailed taxonomy). The private sector can provide financing to companies (both private firms and wholly or partially state-owned enterprises) that provide infrastructure services or invest in several infrastructure projects (corporate balance sheet financing). They can also use special purpose vehicles associated with specific standalone infrastructure projects, the cash flow proceeds from which are the sole source of recourse/repayment (project finance). In both cases, financing can occur through lending (via loans or bonds, often with varying degrees of subordination/seniority or convertibility into equity) or equity.[3]

Balance sheet financing has been more common for utilities, ports, electricity generation, and waste management. The use of project finance has been primarily for capital-intensive projects with highly specific characteristics, such as airports, highways, bridges, tunnels, and metro lines. Indeed, transportation has been the most popular sector for public-private partnerships (PPPs)—arrangements in which the private sector supplies infrastructure assets and services traditionally provided by governments, through concessions or operating leases, in most cases involving a special

---

3. In project finance, debt instruments have historically accounted for 70–90 percent of total capitalization (OECD 2015b). Loans (mostly from banks) have represented more than 80 percent of total debt project finance (AFME 2015).

purpose vehicle.[4] Under this kind of arrangement, a private company builds, maintains, and sometimes operates an asset like a road. In return, the government typically agrees to pay the company for its costs over 20 or 30 years or allows the company to collect user fees.

The popularity of PPPs in transportation reflects three interrelated factors (Akitoby, Hemming, and Schwartz 2007). First, many roads, railways, and ports have high economic rates of return and are therefore attractive to the private sector. Second, user charges are often feasible and desirable. Third, transportation projects have a better-developed market for bundling construction with the provision of related services (for example, construction and operation and maintenance of a toll road).

Programs for PPPs have been well-established in several countries (including Chile, Ireland, Mexico, and the United Kingdom) since the 1990s.[5] Total new investment commitments to private infrastructure projects (in all sectors) for that sample were estimated at more than $110 billion in 2015 (World Bank 2015).

Only a small share of infrastructure financing has come from institutional investors (pension funds, insurance companies, mutual funds, sovereign wealth funds), despite the long-term nature of infrastructure-related projects and institutional investors' needs for long-term assets. In view of rising infrastructure needs and pressures on banks to rebuild their capital and liquidity buffers, various proposals and initiatives have been put forward to tap these underutilized financing resources for infrastructure projects. In particular, the G-20 and the OECD (www.oecd.org/finance/lti) have initiated a dialogue on how to develop the equity market for investments in infrastructure and to promote the use of project bonds as a complement to syndicated loans for project finance.

In recent years a market has developed for institutional investors to coinvest in infrastructure projects (OECD 2015b). A large institutional investor performs due diligence on an investment project and organizes a syndicate, retaining a percentage of each loan in its loan portfolio and selling the remaining portion to other investors (as in syndicated commercial loans). Through this mechanism institutional investors can build diversified portfolios.

"Infrastructure investment platforms" set up by multilateral and regional development banks could tap the funds and expertise of private

---

4. Other sectors where PPPs have long been popular are hospitals, schools, and prisons. PPPs in energy, especially renewables such as solar and wind, have experienced rapid growth in recent years (World Bank 2015).

5. Detailed information on PPPs, including individual projects, is available from the World Bank (http://ppi.worldbank.org/data) for 139 emerging-market economies.

and public sectors for infrastructure investment. The development banks, some of which have decades of experience in assessing and financing infrastructure projects, could provide a seal of approval for projects and thus attract private coinvestors.

The platforms could help mobilize private funds from institutional investors or sovereign wealth funds through three mechanisms:

- providing funding as well as guarantees, thereby sharing the risk with the government and private investors,

- providing expertise in preparing and evaluating infrastructure projects, and

- acting as third-party monitors, taming opportunistic government administrations, with which they have long-term relationships, and helping ensure that private investors do not fund overly optimistic projects in the expectation that the government would ultimately bail out the projects if they fail. For their part, private investors would help ensure that projects supported by governments or developments banks are not politically motivated.

Thus, adding to the financial firepower of multilateral and regional development banks—both existing and new—can not only boost their traditional role as lenders to governments for infrastructure investment, but also enhance their indirect impact as catalysts for private investment.

New financing institutions have been developed in the past few years. The Asian Infrastructure Investment Bank, launched by China in 2013, has 57 founding members and prospective capital of about $100 billion. The Silk Road Fund, which China established in 2014, has $40 billion, which it plans to use to increase trade and transport links along the ancient Silk Road. Both institutions have the potential to play significant roles, as long as they adhere to international norms in lending, including ensuring transparent processes, creating a level playing field among firms bidding for projects, and providing incentives for projects to preserve natural resources and limit risks to climate change (see Djankov and Miner 2016).

Other potentially useful measures to facilitate institutional investors' participation in financing infrastructure involve relaxing some aspects of their prudential regulation. In some countries regulators impose limits on institutional investors' ability to finance infrastructure projects or on the share of assets invested abroad, especially in emerging-market economies deemed too risky. Given the excellent fit between the maturities of infrastructure assets and institutional investors' liabilities, regulators should consider relaxing such prudential limits.

Managing the Risks to the Public Sector from Private Sector Financing

When infrastructure projects are financed through PPPs, some accounting systems make it possible to postpone recording the entire construction cost until project completion (in contrast, traditionally procured projects financed by the government are recorded during construction) (Funke, Irwin, and Rial 2013). Moreover, contingent obligations stemming from guarantees are seldom captured in governments' fiscal accounts at the time they are incurred.

In a PPP contract, government entities may provide private concessionaires with guarantees against shortfalls in revenues or losses from exchange rate fluctuations. If these risks materialize—because traffic projections prove too optimistic or the domestic currency depreciates more than expected, for example—the government ends up footing a large portion of the bill. Such risks are real. During the 1990s, for instance, calls on demand guarantees related to PPPs in power, telecommunications, and toll roads in Colombia added cumulative payments equivalent to 2 percent of that country's annual GDP by 2004 (Cebotari et al. 2009). Substantial obligations on PPP contracts in power plants and roads became due in Indonesia, Malaysia, and Thailand in the late 1990s, partly as a result of the decline in demand associated with the Asian financial crisis. In the early 2000s, the governments of several advanced countries provided equity contributions in, operating subsidies to, or full bailouts and renationalization of transportation infrastructure—in some cases costing as much as 0.5 percent of GDP for individual projects.

With the global economic and financial crisis that began in 2008, the cost of earlier commitments proved even greater in some countries. In Portugal, where PPPs were an important source of financing in the late 1990s and early 2000s, calls on government guarantees contributed the equivalent of 10–15 percentage points of GDP to the rise in public debt during the three years following the onset of the crisis (IMF 2013).

With rising public debts and growing infrastructure needs, policymakers may be tempted to use PPPs not only because private sector expertise can provide efficiency gains but also because it may be possible to conceal from citizens, investors, and the government the true impact of PPPs on the state of the public finances. Against this background, it is particularly important for governments to avoid using accounting devices that can obfuscate the public costs of investment. Transparency at all stages of infrastructure projects—from selection to implementation and recording of final costs—helps level the playing field for all companies, increasing the chances that governments obtain the best value for money.

Successful PPPs require good monitoring and disclosure practices, including systems for making public accurate and timely information on contracts (through a statement of fiscal risks submitted to parliament alongside the budget documents, for example). They also require the management of risks.[6] Mechanisms for doing so include (1) establishing a dedicated unit at the ministry of finance that assesses whether projects put forward by line ministries are affordable and provide value for money, (2) having parliament scrutinize and approve contracts, (3) setting caps on the total risk exposure from PPPs, (4) integrating guarantee issuance decisions with the budget process to ensure that projects compete on a more equal footing regardless of whether they are financed through guarantees or expenditure appropriations, and (5) budgeting for expected calls on contingent obligations or establishing notional or actual contingency funds.

To avoid postponing the recording of firm obligations associated with PPPs, governments can prepare audited financial statements—income statements, cash-flow statements, and balance sheets—that meet international accounting standards. Where accounting standards do not require recording all prospective PPP-related fiscal obligations, such "PPP debt" should be recorded in documentation provided to parliament.

Improving Public Procurement Procedures and Preventing Corruption and Fraud

Regardless of the source of financing, ensuring that infrastructure projects yield good value for money requires good public procurement procedures.[7] Such policies are crucial because of the vast potential for corruption. Indeed, OECD (2014) finds that more than half of foreign bribery cases occurred in public procurement. Transparency and good record-keeping are critical at all procurement phases, including pre-tendering (evaluation needs reports, market studies, establishment of criteria); tendering (contract requirements, bid analysis, and application of criteria); and post-

---

6. A "Project Checklist for Public-Private Partnerships," published in 2015 by the World Bank and the OECD, describes desirable project features and assessment or implementation processes, including broad government and stakeholder support; clear and stable regulations; transparent information; and the assessment of costs and benefits, fiscal consequences, and risk sharing.

7. Many sources are available for policymakers. They include *The Procurement Handbook* (Dimitri, Piga, and Spagnolo 2006); the OECD's toolbox of guidelines and checklists (www. oecd.org/governance/procurement/toolbox); and OECD (2016), which provides both general principles and good-practice examples of public investment integrity and transparency frameworks, codes of conduct, and whistleblower protection.

award (observations during contract performance, price changes, supplementary work).

To deter and detect corruption and fraud, governments need to establish mechanisms through which whistleblowers can alert the authorities of wrongdoing. They can encourage whistleblowing by offering large rewards and protection against retaliation.

Creating a hospitable business environment and reducing the scope for the abuse of public office are key to fostering private participation in public infrastructure projects and attracting private investment more generally. Corruption, inefficient judicial systems, and weak rule of law impede private investment and economic growth (Mauro 1995). Addressing these problems and lowering administrative and regulatory barriers would help attract private actors. (For a discussion of these issues, see Mauro 2007 and Kaufmann 2015.)

Creating Incentives for Climate-Friendly Infrastructure

The key battlegrounds in the fight against climate change over the next two decades will be the emerging-market economies. Spending on transportation will rise far more rapidly in these economies (a projected cumulative increase of $8.4 trillion between 2015 and 2035) than in the advanced economies ($4.3 trillion). By the end of the projection period, transportation spending will be higher in the emerging-market economies ($12.3 trillion) than in the advanced economies ($10.3 trillion).

Efforts to limit global temperature increases—such as the agreement reached at the conference on climate change in Paris in December 2015—will be successful only if they curb emissions from rising consumption by residents of emerging-market economies. Progress will require choosing subways over roads for in-city commuting, trains over cars for longer-distance travel, and renewable energy over coal (at least in the absence of carbon capture and storage) for power generation.[8] Although policymakers in emerging-market economies will make the key decisions, policymakers in the advanced economies can play a useful role by providing the right incentives to steer their decisions toward climate-friendly options.

Beyond taking action at home and financing research and development of green technologies, the advanced economies can also help multilateral and regional development banks as well as export credit agencies provide financial incentives for choosing climate-friendly infrastructure

---

8. Carbon capture and storage is the process of capturing waste carbon dioxide from fossil fuel power plants and storing it where it will not enter the atmosphere, normally in an underground geological formation.

projects. All countries should ensure that procurement of infrastructure projects is internationally open and transparent and uses the most efficient technologies.

Domestic policy actions that curb energy use include higher taxation of, and lower subsidies on, fossil fuels and the replacement of subsidies with targeted interventions to protect the most vulnerable people (see Lagarde and Kim 2015, OECD 2015c). Excessively low energy prices contribute to premature deaths from local pollution, exacerbate congestion, and increase greenhouse gas emissions. Energy subsidies impose fiscal costs and discourage investment in energy efficiency and renewable energy technologies.[9] Governments often resort to such subsidies under the guise of reducing inequality, but fuel subsidies are an inefficient way to support low-income households. Indeed, such policies are regressive, because better-off households capture most of the benefits (poor households in developing countries seldom own cars, and they consume less energy). Most aspects of energy tax/subsidy policies are in the domestic domain, but in some cases (such as higher taxation of international air travel), international coordination is required and warranted.

---

9. Coady et al. (2015) estimate total global post-tax consumer subsidies at $4.9 trillion (6.5 percent of GDP). Public discourse often refers to pretax consumer subsidies—the gap between the cost of supplying energy and the price paid by firms and households. A few studies (for example, OECD 2015d) also include producer subsidies, which reflect subsidized inputs, preferential treatment, or direct budget transfers to energy producers. Post-tax consumer subsidies are the relevant concept: They arise when the price paid by consumers is below the cost of supplying energy plus a corrective tax that reflects the environmental damage caused by energy consumption plus an additional consumption tax that should be applied to all goods and services.

8

Challenges from Rising Consumption in the Next 20 Years

The combination of population growth and the growth in consumption is a danger that we are not prepared for and something we will need global cooperation on.

—Maurice Strong

In the next 20 years, the global consumption landscape will change as vast numbers of people in emerging-market economies increasingly share the benefits of economic growth. The center of gravity for business opportunities will shift further toward China, India, and other parts of South and East Asia, as well as Sub-Saharan Africa.

In the baseline projections, the number of people worldwide with per capita incomes below $2,000 a year will decline by more than 1.1 billion over the next 20 years, despite overall population growth. The number of people with incomes of $2,000–$6,000 will increase by almost 700 million; they will be able to afford basic consumer goods, such as a refrigerator, for the first time, and to eat more meat and fish on a regular basis. The number of people with incomes of $6,000–$20,000 will rise by a little over a billion; many of them will purchase their first car. The number of people earning $20,000 and above will increase by almost 800 million; many will fly for leisure for the first time.

By 2035 global inequality will be lower than it is now. The global Gini index is projected to decline to 66.6 in 2035, from 69.1 in 2015 and 73.8 in 2003. The 90:10 ratio will fall to 25.3 in 2035, down from 28.5 in 2015. Consumption patterns will become more similar, as more people in emerging-market economies become able to afford consumer goods and services currently associated with rich countries.

These achievements notwithstanding, 400 million people will still live in absolute poverty, and inequality will remain high—both globally and within many countries. With growing awareness of income disparities, demands for greater equality within and across countries may intensify, manifesting through the political process and migration pressures.

Higher consumption of goods and services improves the well-being of vast segments of the world's population. But rising consumption and its concentration in transportation, an energy-intensive sector, will also put a strain on natural resources and the climate. As incomes rise, people increase their spending on transportation more than proportionately. Spending on transportation is projected to quadruple in India and China, closely followed by Sub-Saharan Africa. Meeting this demand could cost $48 trillion globally for new roads and railways alone.

Addressing these trends will require policy action at the domestic and global levels. Actions by policymakers, business leaders, and investors will determine whether the changing consumption landscape results in sustainable and equitable improvements in well-being.

Reducing Inequality

Although global inequality is projected to decline, vast differences between rich and poor individuals will persist two decades from now. Policymakers should seek to reduce inequality because doing so is morally right and because it contributes to social peace.

The scope for policies to reduce global inequality by redistributing income across national borders is limited. The main vehicle for doing so has been foreign aid. Such aid has been useful during humanitarian crises. Its effectiveness in promoting longer-term growth, however, has been hotly debated (see Edwards 2014 for a review of studies on aid effectiveness).

Global inequality can decline more rapidly than projected if inequality within countries is reduced, as illustrated in chapter 4. Policies to do so are primarily under the purview of national governments. Direct redistribution within countries has traditionally been accomplished through a mix of progressive taxation and subsidies/transfers (preferably means-tested). Some experts contend that the traditional approach is insufficient, that additional policies should aim at achieving a more equal distribution of market income (income before taxes and benefits). Anthony B. Atkinson (2015, 113) suggests that "today's high level of inequality can be effectively reduced only by tackling inequality in the marketplace." Governments need to take distributional effects into account when designing laws and regulations, including innovation policy, antitrust policy, trade union legislation, and wage regulations and bargaining systems.

Increasing global integration also calls for governments to act together. Global coordination of tax administration and tax policy can make a significant contribution to reducing inequality, both within and across countries. The recent G-20/OECD initiative to stem tax avoidance by global corporations through "base erosion and profit shifting" seeks to ensure that global corporations pay a fair share of their profits in the countries where such profits are generated. Efforts to soften bank secrecy laws to permit sharing of information with foreign tax authorities seek to reduce tax evasion across national borders. Ensuring that global corporations and high net worth individuals contribute their fair share to tax revenues would reduce the accumulation of riches in the hands of a few and provide additional resources for governments, which they could redistribute domestically or invest in ways that foster economic growth to the benefit of broader segments of the population. A global wealth tax would prevent a "race to the bottom" by countries competing to attract mobile millionaires (see, for example, Piketty 2014).

Beyond efforts at redistribution of incomes, rapid growth in the emerging-market economies will be a crucial determinant of the speed at which global inequality is reduced. To that end, adequate financing of infrastructure investment will be key.

Boosting Infrastructure Investment

As a larger share of the global population meets its basic necessities for food, clothing, and shelter, demand for transportation will soar, particularly in emerging-market economies. Increased mobility can foster economic growth in emerging-market economies, further reducing global inequality.

Policymakers should start planning for major new investment early on, so that it can be adequately financed while keeping in check the risks to public finances and the possibility of waste or corruption. Fiscal policy is the right place to start, through higher revenues and expenditure reallocation toward public investment. Ensuring that both new investment and maintenance spending are fully reflected in medium-term fiscal frameworks would be helpful.

For fast-growing emerging-market economies in particular, the scale of financing cannot be met without much-expanded participation by the private sector. To foster private investor participation in infrastructure, governments need to create a stable regulatory environment and an open and transparent procurement system, which curbs the scope for corruption. Measures in these areas are especially important in emerging-market economies, where the needs are greatest and institutional quality weaker than in advanced economies.

A potentially vast increase in financing from the private sector could come from institutional investors such as pension funds. Possible measures include relaxing the prudential requirements for such investors to participate in infrastructure projects (both domestically and abroad) and setting up coinvestment platforms with multilateral and regional development banks, which could provide a seal of approval for projects.

Governments should not use private participation to postpone the recording of related fiscal obligations or underrecord the fiscal risks associated with providing guarantees to private partners. Procedures should be in place to monitor, disclose, and manage such fiscal risks.

Another way in which policymakers can ensure that spending on transportation and infrastructure investment experience healthy growth is to maintain and deepen openness to international trade. Investment has a higher import content than private consumption or government spending, and machinery and transportation equipment is the largest component of goods trade (for empirical evidence, see Bussière et al. 2013 and Freund 2016).

Preserving the Sustainability of Consumption Growth through International Cooperation

As people consume more and shift their spending toward goods and services that use more energy, the question of how rapid growth can be sustained without disastrous consequences for scarce natural resources and the global climate gains renewed urgency. This is not the first time that Malthusian concerns emerge about the sustainability of economic and population growth. For the most part, such concerns have proven unwarranted.[1]

But the jury is still out. The OECD (2015e) estimates that—absent new measures—worsening climate change, urban air pollution, water shortages, and biodiversity loss would impose massive costs on people, especially the poor, and the global economy.

The resourcefulness and technological innovations that have led mankind to overcome the Malthusian trap have been driven by individual thirst for profit and survival. When food became scarce, people developed more resistant crops and more efficient farming techniques—and some made a profit doing so.

---

1. Thomas Malthus (1798) considered that, with population growing "geometrically" in the absence of constraints and food supply growing "arithmetically," population growth would necessarily be kept in check by misery felt by "a large portion of mankind." With the global population explosion that began in the aftermath of World War II (which increased the population from 2.5 billion in 1950 to 7 billion in 2011), Malthusian fears resurfaced. Pioneering interdisciplinary books on sustainability (such as Meadows et al. 1972), including those prepared under the aegis of the Club of Rome, became popular in the 1970s (for a survey and several additional citations, see Rome 2015). Scientific advances led to a greater understanding of the threat to the planet from human activity.

This time may be different. Many of today's problems, such as climate change, involve powerful externalities (see Helbling 2010); individually desirable or profitable behavior imposes a cost on society as a whole, including carbon emissions resulting from simple everyday actions such as driving. Against that background, free markets and the profit motive alone cannot provide the solution. Correcting externalities will require public policies such as carbon taxation.

When externalities take place across national borders, international coordination of policies becomes crucial. No government wants to be the first to ask its citizens to accept lower economic growth or higher taxation, even if these actions would reduce the chances of environmental disaster affecting everyone on the planet. International agreements such as the one reached at the Paris conference in December 2015—whereby all countries committed themselves to carrying out national action plans to limit carbon emissions—are a good starting point but may prove insufficient as well as difficult to monitor and implement.

Part of the motivation for this book is to provide analytically grounded estimates and projections that may sensitize readers to the scale of the forthcoming pressures from rising and changing consumption to be faced by governments and the global community—and to make the case for greater international cooperation in these areas.

Several policy measures would help steer consumption toward cleaner options:

- Cut energy subsidies and increase carbon taxation (see, for example, Lagarde and Kim 2015, OECD 2015c). Although much can be accomplished domestically in this area, some actions require international coordination. Such actions include, for example, higher taxation of international air travel (whether through taxes on jet fuel or airline tickets), which was not covered by Kyoto emission limits, or its inclusion in emission limits.

- Finance research and development of green technologies and a global climate adaptation fund, with the advanced economies making the largest contributions.

- Regional and multilateral development banks as well as export credit agencies should provide financial incentives for choosing climate-friendly infrastructure, including in the transportation sector.

- Procurement of infrastructure projects should be internationally open and transparent to facilitate the use of the most efficient technologies worldwide.

Rising consumption, particularly in emerging-market economies, will improve well-being for billions of people in the next two decades. But these opportunities will come with dangers. Improvements in global inequality may be too slow to avoid political backlash. Failure to secure financing for needed infrastructure may cause economic growth to grind to a halt. Lack of international coordination to curb climate change could imperil the planet's survival. Policymakers need to take action urgently to face these seemingly slow-moving trends before it is too late.

References

Abizadeh, Arash. 2007. Cooperation, Pervasive Impact, and Coercion: On the Scope (Not Site) of Distributive Justice. *Philosophy and Public Affairs* 35, no. 4: 318–58.

Acosta-Ormaechea, Santiago, and Atsuyoshi Morozumi. 2013. *Can a Government Enhance Long-Run Growth by Changing the Composition of Public Expenditure?* IMF Working Paper 13/162. Washington: International Monetary Fund.

AFME (Association for Financial Markets in Europe). 2015. *Guide to Infrastructure Financing.* Zurich.

Airbus. 2015. *Global Market Forecast 2015–2034.* Available at www.airbus.com/company/market/forecast/.

Akitoby, Bernardin, Richard Hemming, and Gerd Schwartz. 2007. Public Investment and Public-Private Partnerships. *IMF Economic Issues* no. 40. Washington: International Monetary Fund.

Anand, Sudhir, and Paul Segal. 2008. What Do We Know about Global Income Inequality? *Journal of Economic Literature* 46, no. 1: 57–94.

Anand, Sudhir, and Paul Segal. 2015. The Global Distribution of Income. In *Handbook of Income Distribution*, ed. Anthony Atkinson and François Bourguignon. Amsterdam: Elsevier.

Anand, Sudhir, and Paul Segal. 2016. *Who Are the Global Top 1%?* Department of Economics Discussion Paper 799. University of Oxford.

Atkinson, Anthony B. 2015. *Inequality: What Can Be Done?* Cambridge, MA: Harvard University Press.

Atkinson, Anthony B., Thomas Piketty, and Emmanuel Saez, eds. 2007. *Top Incomes over the Twentieth Century: A Contrast between Continental European and English-Speaking Countries.* Oxford: Oxford University Press.

Atkinson, Anthony B., Thomas Piketty, and Emmanuel Saez, eds. 2010. *Top Incomes: A Global Perspective.* Oxford: Oxford University Press.

Atkinson, Anthony B., Thomas Piketty, and Emmanuel Saez. 2011. Top Incomes in the Long Run of History. *Journal of Economic Literature* 49, no. 1: 3–71.

Barro, Robert J. 2000. Inequality and Growth in a Panel of Countries. *Journal of Economic Growth* 5: 5–35.

Bhalla, Surjit S. 2002. *Imagine There's No Country: Poverty, Inequality, and Growth in the Era of Globalization.* Washington: Institute for International Economics.

Bhandari, Rabindra, Gyan Pradhan, and Mukti Upadhyay. 2010. Another Empirical Look at the Kuznets Curve. *International Journal of Economic Sciences and Applied Research* 3, no. 2: 7–19.

Blake, Michael. 2001. Distributive Justice, State Coercion, and Autonomy. *Philosophy and Public Affairs* 30, no. 3: 257–96.

Blake, Michael, and Patrick Taylor Smith. 2015. International Distributive Justice. *Stanford Encyclopedia of Philosophy.* Available at http://plato.stanford.edu/archives/spr2015/entries/international-justice/.

Bongaarts, John, and Rodolfo A. Bulatao, eds. 2000. *Beyond Six Billion: Forecasting the World's Population.* Washington: National Academy Press.

Bound, John, Charles Brown, and Nancy Mathiowetz. 2001. Measurement Error in Survey Data. In *Handbook of Econometrics,* vol. 5, ed. J. J. Heckman and E. Leamer, 3705–843. Amsterdam: North-Holland.

Bourguignon, François, and Christian Morrisson. 2002. Inequality among World Citizens: 1820–1992. *American Economic Review* 92, no. 4: 727–44.

Brainerd, Elizabeth, and David M. Cutler. 2005. Autopsy on an Empire: The Mortality Crisis in Russia and the Former Soviet Union. *Journal of Economic Perspectives* 19, no. 1: 107–30.

Bricker, Jesse, Alice M. Henriques, Jake A. Krimmel, and John E. Sabelhaus. 2015. *Measuring Income and Wealth at the Top Using Administrative and Survey Data.* Finance and Economics Discussion Series. Washington: Federal Reserve Board.

Bussière, Matthieu, Giovanni Callegari, Fabio Ghironi, Giulia Sestieri, and Norihiko Yama. 2013. Estimating Trade Elasticities: Demand Composition and the Trade Collapse of 2008–09. *American Economic Journal: Macroeconomics* 5: 118–51.

Caney, Simon. 2005. *Justice Beyond Borders.* Oxford: Oxford University Press.

Case, Anne, and Angus Deaton. 2015. Rising Morbidity and Mortality in Midlife among White Non-Hispanic Americans in the 21st Century. *Proceedings of the National Academy of Sciences of the United States of America* 112, no. 49: 15078–83. Available at www.pnas.org/content/112/49/15078.

Cavallero, Eric. 2010. Cohesion, Equality and the International Property Regime. *Journal of Political Philosophy* 18: 16–31.

Cebotari, Aliona, Jeffrey Davis, Lusine Lusinyan, Amine Mati, Paolo Mauro, Murray Petrie, and Ricardo Velloso. 2009. *Fiscal Risks: Sources, Disclosure, and Management.* Fiscal Affairs Department Paper. Washington: International Monetary Fund.

Chamon, Marcos, Paolo Mauro, and Yohei Okawa. 2008. Mass Car Ownership in the Emerging Market Giants. *Economic Policy* (April): 243–96.

Chen, Shaohua, and Martin Ravallion. 2010. The Developing World Is Poorer than We Thought, but No Less Successful in the Fight against Poverty. *Quarterly Journal of Economics* 125, no. 4: 1577–625.

Chotikapanich, Duangkamon, Rebecca Valenzuela, and D. S. Prasada Rao. 1997. Global and Regional Inequality in the Distribution of Income: Estimation with Limited and Incomplete Data. *Empirical Economics* 22, no. 4: 533–46.

Clemens, Michael A. 2014. Does Development Reduce Migration? In *International Handbook on Migration and Economic Development*, ed. Robert E. B. Lucas. Cheltenham, UK: Edward Elgar Publishing.

Cline, William R. 2004. *Trade Policy and Global Poverty*. Washington: Institute for International Economics.

Coady, David, Ian W. H. Parry, Louis Sears, and Baoping Shang. 2015. *How Large Are Global Energy Subsidies?* IMF Working Paper 15/105. Washington: International Monetary Fund.

Cohen, Joshua, and Charles Sabel. 2009. Extram Republicam Nulla Justicia? *Philosophy and Public Affairs* 34: 147–75.

Cowell, Frank A. 2011. *Measuring Inequality*. Oxford: Oxford University Press.

Credit Suisse. 2013. *Sugar Consumption at a Crossroads*. Zurich: Credit Suisse Research Institute. Available at https://publications.credit-suisse.com/tasks/render/file/index.cfm?fileid=780BF4A8-B3D1-13A0-D2514E21EFFB0479.

Credit Suisse. 2014. *Global Wealth Report*. Zurich: Credit Suisse Research Institute.

Dargay, Joyce, Dermot Gately, and Martin Sommer. 2007. Vehicle Ownership and Income Growth, Worldwide: 1960–2030. *Energy Journal* 28, no. 4: 143–70.

Davies, James B., Susanna Sandström, Anthony Shorrocks, and Edward N. Wolff. 2011. The Level and Distribution of Global Household Wealth. *Economic Journal* 121, no. 551: 223–54.

Deaton, Angus. 2005. Measuring Poverty in a Growing World (or Measuring Growth in a Poor World). *Review of Economics and Statistics* 87, no. 1: 1–19.

Deaton, Angus. 2013. *The Great Escape: Health, Wealth, and the Origins of Inequality*. Princeton, NJ: Princeton University Press.

Deininger, Klaus, and Lyn Squire. 1998. New Ways of Looking at Old Issues: Inequality and Growth. *Journal of Development Economics* 57, no. 2: 259–87.

Desbordes, Rodolphe, and Vincenzo Verardi. 2012. Refitting the Kuznets Curve. *Economic Letters* 116: 258–61.

Dimitri, Nicola, Gustavo Piga, and Giancarlo Spagnolo, eds. 2006. *Handbook of Procurement*. Cambridge: Cambridge University Press.

Djankov, Simeon, and Sean Miner, eds. 2016. *China's Belt and Road Initiative: Motives, Scope, and Challenges*. PIIE Briefing 16-2. Washington: Peterson Institute for International Economics.

Dobbs, Richard, Herbert Pohl, Diaan-Yi Lin, Jan Mischke, Nicklas Garemo, Jimmy Hexter, Stefan Matzinger, Robert Palter, and Rushad Nanavatty. 2013. *Infrastructure Productivity: How to Save $1 Trillion a Year*. Washington: McKinsey Global Institute.

Dobbs, Richard, Jaana Remes, James Manyika, Charles Roxburgh, Sven Smit, and Fabian Schaer. 2012. *Urban World: Cities and the Rise of the Consumer Class*. Washington: McKinsey Global Institute.

Dollar, David, Tatjana Kleineberg, and Aart Kraay. 2013. *Growth Still Is Good for the Poor*. Policy Research Working Paper 6568. Washington: World Bank.

Dollar, David, Tatjana Kleineberg, and Aart Kraay. 2014. *Growth, Inequality, and Social Welfare: Cross-Country Evidence.* Policy Research Working Paper 6842. Washington: World Bank.

Dowrick, Steve, and Muhammad Akmal. 2005. Contradictory Trends in Global Income Inequality: A Tale of Two Biases. *Review of Income and Wealth* 51, no. 2: 201–29.

Drummond, Paulo, Vimal Thakoor, and Shu Yu. 2014. *Africa Rising: Harnessing the Demographic Dividend.* IMF Working Paper 14/143. Washington: International Monetary Fund.

Du S., T. A. Mroz, F. Zhai, and B. M. Pokin. 2004. Rapid Income Growth Adversely Affects Diet Quality in China. *Social Science and Medicine* 59, no. 7: 1505–515.

Dulac, John. 2013. *Global Land Transport Infrastructure Requirements: Estimating Road and Railway Infrastructure Capacity and Costs to 2050.* Paris: International Energy Agency. Available at www.iea.org/publications/freepublications/publication/TransportInfrastructureInsights_FINAL_WEB.pdf.

Easterly, William, and Sergio Rebelo. 1993. Fiscal Policy and Economic Growth. *Journal of Monetary Economics* 32: 417–58.

Edward, Peter, and Andy Sumner. 2013. *Inequality from a Global Perspective: An Alternative Approach.* ECINEQ Working Paper Series 2013-302. Verona, Italy: Society for the Study of Economic Inequality.

Edwards, Sebastian. 2014. *Economic Development and the Effectiveness of Foreign Aid: A Historical Perspective.* NBER Working Paper 20685. Cambridge, MA: National Bureau of Economic Research.

Engel, Ernst. 1857. Die Productions und Consumptionsverhaeltnisse des Koenigresichs Sachsen. *Zeitschrift des Statistischen Bureaus des Koniglich Sachsischen Ministeriums des Inneren,* 8 und 9. Reprinted in the appendix to Engel (1895).

Engel, Ernst. 1895. Die Lebenskosten belgischer Arbeiter-Familien, fruher and jetzt. *International Statistical Institute Bulletin* 9: 1–74.

Engström, Per, and Bertil Holmlund. 2009. Tax Evasion and Self-Employment in a High-Tax Country: Evidence from Sweden. *Applied Economics* 41, no. 19: 2419–30.

Fernald, John G. 1999. Roads to Prosperity? Assessing the Link between Public Capital and Productivity. *American Economic Review* 89, no. 3: 619–38.

Fishlow, Albert. 1965. *American Railroads and the Transformation of the Ante-bellum Economy.* Cambridge, MA: Harvard University Press.

Fogel, Robert. 1964. *Railroads and American Economic Growth: Essays in Econometric History.* Baltimore, MD: Johns Hopkins University Press.

Foley, Jonathan. 2014. A Five-Step Plan to Feed the World. *National Geographic* (May): 26–59. Available at www.nationalgeographic.com/foodfeatures/feeding-9-billion/.

Forbes, Kristen. 2000. A Reassessment of the Relationship between Inequality and Growth. *American Economic Review* 90, no. 4: 869–87.

Freeman, Samuel. 2006. The Law of Peoples, Social Cooperation, Human Rights, and Distributive Justice. *Social Philosophy and Policy* 23, no. 1: 29–68.

Freund, Caroline. 2016. Global Trade Growth: Slow but Steady. In *Reality Check for the Global Economy,* ed. Olivier Blanchard and Adam Posen. PIIE Briefing 16-3. Washington: Peterson Institute for International Economics.

Funke, Katja, Tim Irwin, and Isabel Rial. 2013. *Budgeting and Reporting for Public-Private Partnerships*. OECD/International Transport Forum Discussion Paper 2013/07. Paris: Organization for Economic Cooperation and Development.

Gordon, Robert. 2015. *The Rise and Fall of American Growth*. Princeton, NJ: Princeton University Press.

Gottschalk, Peter, and Minh Huynh. 2010. Are Earnings Inequality and Mobility Overstated? The Impact of Nonclassical Measurement Error. *Review of Economics and Statistics* 92, no. 2: 302–15.

Grondin, C., and S. Michaud. 1994. *Data Quality of Income Data Using Computer-Assisted Interview: The Experience of the Canadian Survey of Labour and Income Dynamics*. Ottawa: Statistics Canada.

Groves, Robert M., and Mick P. Couper. 1998. *Nonresponse in Household Interview Surveys*. New York: Wiley.

Gyomai, György, and Peter van de Ven. 2014. The Non-Observed Economy in the System of National Accounts. *OECD Statistics Brief* 18: 1–12.

Helbling, Thomas. 2010. What Are Externalities? *Finance and Development* (December): 48–49.

Hellebrandt, Tomas. 2014. *Income Inequality Developments in the Great Recession*. PIIE Policy Brief 14-3. Washington: Peterson Institute for International Economics.

Hellebrandt, Tomas, and Paolo Mauro. 2015. *The Future of Worldwide Income Distribution*. PIIE Working Paper 15-7. Washington: Peterson Institute for International Economics.

Higgins, M., and J. Williamson. 2002. Explaining Inequality the World Round: Cohort Size, Kuznets Curves, and Openness. *Southeast Asian Studies* 40, no. 3: 269–88.

Ho, Giang, and Paolo Mauro. 2016. Growth: Now and Forever? *IMF Economic Review* 64, no. 35: 26–47.

Hurst, Eric, Geng Li, and Benjamin Pugsley. 2010. *Are Household Surveys Like Tax Forms? Evidence from Income Underreporting of the Self-Employed*. NBER Working Paper 16527. Cambridge, MA: National Bureau of Economic Research.

IEA (International Energy Agency). 2015. *World Energy Outlook*. Paris.

IMF (International Monetary Fund). 2013. *Growth-Friendly, Equitable, and Sustainable Fiscal Reform in Portugal*. IMF Country Report 13/19. Washington.

IMF (International Monetary Fund). 2014. Is It Time for an Infrastructure Push? The Macroeconomic Effects of Public Investment. *World Economic Outlook* (October). Washington.

IMF (International Monetary Fund). 2015. *Making Public Investment More Efficient*. Washington. Available at www.imf.org/external/np/pp/eng/2015/061115.pdf.

International Road Federation. 2015. *World Road Statistics*. Geneva.

Jenkins, Stephen P. 2014. *World Income Inequality Databases: An Assessment of WIID and SWIID*. IZA Discussion Paper 8501. Bonn: Institute for the Study of Labor (IZA). Available at http://ssrn.com/abstract=2505363.

Johansson, Edvard. 2005. An Estimate of Self-Employment Income Underreporting in Finland. *Nordic Journal of Political Economy* 31, no. 1: 99–109.

Johansson, Åsa, Yvan Guillemette, Fabrice Murtin, David Turner, Giuseppe Nicoletti, Christine de la Maisonneuve, Phillip Bagnoli, Guillaume Bousquet and Francesca Spinelli. 2013. *Long-Term Growth Scenarios*. Economics Department Working Paper no. 1000. Paris: Organization for Economic Cooperation and Development.

Johansson, Åsa, Yvan Guillemette, Fabrice Murtin, David Turner, Giuseppe Nicoletti, Christine de la Maisonneuve, Phillip Bagnoli, Guillaume Bousquet and Francesca Spinelli. 2013. *Long-Term Growth Scenarios*. Economics Department Working Paper no. 1000. Paris: Organization for Economic Cooperation and Development.

Jones, Charles. 2015. *The Facts of Economic Growth*. NBER Working Paper 21142. Cambridge, MA: National Bureau of Economic Research.

Kaufmann, Daniel. 2015. Corruption Matters. *Finance & Development* 52, no. 3: 20–23.

Kharas, Homi. 2010. *The Emerging Middle Class in Developing Countries*. OECD Development Centre Working Paper 285. Paris: Organization for Economic Cooperation and Development.

Kim, Bonggeun, John Gibson, and Chul Chung. 2009. *Using Panel Data to Exactly Estimate Income Under-Reporting by Self-Employed*. KIEP Working Paper 09-02. Seoul: Korea Institute for International Economic Policy. Available at http://acjer.eaber.org/sites/default/files/documents/KIEP_Kim_2009.pdf.

Korinek, A., J. A. Mistiaen, and M. Ravallion. 2006. Survey Nonresponse and the Distribution of Income. *Journal of Economic Inequality* 4, no. 1: 33–55.

Kukk, Merike, and Karsten Staehr. 2013. *Income Underreporting by Households with Business Income. Evidence from Estonia*. Eesti Pank Working Paper 6/2013. Tallinn: Bank of Estonia.

Kunzig, Robert. 2014. Carnivore's Dilemma. *National Geographic* (July). Available at www.nationalgeographic.com/foodfeatures/meat.

Kuznets, Simon. 1955. Economic Growth and Income Inequality. *American Economic Review* 45 (March): 1–28.

Lagarde, Christine, and Jim Yong Kim. 2015. *The Path to Carbon Pricing*. Project Syndicate. Available at www.project-syndicate.org/commentary/carbon-pricing-fiscal-policy-by-christine-lagarde-and-jim-yong-kim-2015-10.

Lahoti, Rahul, Arjun Jayadev, and Sanjay G. Reddy. 2016. *The Global Consumption and Income Project (GCIP): An Overview*. Available at http://papers.ssrn.com/sol3/papers.cfm?abstract_id=2480636.

Lakner, Christoph, and Branko Milanović. 2013. *Global Income Distribution: From the Fall of the Berlin Wall to the Great Recession*. World Bank Working Paper 6719. Washington: World Bank.

Lakner, Christoph, and Branko Milanović. 2016. Global Income Distribution: From the Fall of the Berlin Wall to the Great Recession. *World Bank Economic Review* 30, no. 2: 203–32.

Lewbel, Arthur. 2006. Engel Curves. *New Palgrave Dictionary of Economics*, 2d ed. Basingstoke, UK: Palgrave Macmillan.

Luxembourg Income Study Database. n.d. Available at www.lisdatacenter.org.

MacIntyre, Alasdair. 1981. *After Virtue*. South Bend, IN: University of Notre Dame Press.

Majevski, John. 2006. Review of Albert Fishlow's *American Railroads and the Transformation of the Antebellum Economy*. Available at http://eh.net/book_reviews/american-railroads-and-the-transformation-of-the-ante-bellum-economy/.

Malthus, Thomas. 1798. *An Essay on the Principle of Population*. London: J. Johnson.

Mauro, Paolo. 1995. Corruption and Growth. *Quarterly Journal of Economics* 110, no. 3: 681–712.

Mauro, Paolo. 1998. Corruption and the Composition of Government Expenditure. *Journal of Public Economics* 69: 263-79.

Mauro, Paolo. 2007. World Bank Researchers and the Study of Corruption. *Brown Journal of World Affairs* 13, no. 2: 67-77.

Meadows, Donella, Dennis Meadows, Jørgen Randers, and William Behrens. 1972. *The Limits to Growth: A Report for the Club of Rome's Project on the Predicament of Mankind*. New York: Universe Books.

Meyer, Bruce D., Wallace K. C. Mok, and James X. Sullivan. 2015. Household Surveys in Crisis. *Journal of Economic Perspectives* 29, no. 4: 199-226.

Milanović, Branko. 2002. True World Income Distribution, 1988 and 1993: First Calculation Based on Household Surveys Alone. *Economic Journal* 112, no. 476: 51-92.

Milanović, Branko. 2005. *Worlds Apart: Measuring International and Global Inequality*. Princeton, NJ: Princeton University Press.

Milanović, Branko. 2015. Global Inequality of Opportunity: How Much of Our Income Is Determined by Where We Live? *Review of Economics and Statistics* 97, no. 2: 452-60.

Milanović, Branko. 2016. *Global Inequality: A New Approach for the Age of Globalization*. Cambridge, MA: Harvard University Press.

Moellendorf, Darrel. 2011. Cosmopolitanism and Compatriot Duties. *The Moralist* 94, no. 4: 535-54.

Mokyr, Joel, Chris Vickers, and Nicolas L. Ziebrath. 2015. The History of Technological Anxiety and the Future of Economic Growth: Is This Time Different? *Journal of Economic Perspectives* 29, no. 3: 31-50.

Murphy, Kevin M., Andrei Shleifer, and Robert W. Vishny. 1989. Industrialization and the Big Push. *Journal of Political Economy* 97, no. 5: 1003-26.

Nagel, Thomas. 2005. The Problem of Global Justice. *Philosophy and Public Affairs* 33: 113-47.

OECD (Organization for Economic Cooperation and Development). 2012. *Strategic Transport Infrastructure Needs in 2030*. Paris. Available at http://dx.doi.org/10.1787/9789264114425-en.

OECD (Organization for Economic Cooperation and Development). 2014. *OECD Foreign Bribery Report: An Analysis of the Crime of Bribery of Foreign Public Officials*. Paris. Available at http://dx.doi.org/10.1787/9789264226616-en.

OECD (Organization for Economic Cooperation and Development). 2015a. *In It Together: Why Less Inequality Benefits All*. Paris.

OECD (Organization for Economic Cooperation and Development). 2015b. *Infrastructure Financing Instruments and Incentives*. Paris.

OECD (Organization for Economic Cooperation and Development). 2015c. *Aligning Policies for a Low-Carbon Economy*. Paris.

OECD (Organization for Economic Cooperation and Development). 2015d. *Companion to the Inventory of Support Measures for Fossil Fuels*. Paris.

OECD (Organization for Economic Cooperation and Development). 2015e. *The Economic Consequences of Climate Change*. Paris.

OECD (Organization for Economic Cooperation and Development). 2016. Integrity Framework for Public Investment. Available at http://dx.doi.org/10.1787/9789264251762-en.

OECD (Organization for Economic Cooperation and Development) and ITF (International Transport Forum). 2015. *ITF Transport Outlook 2015*. Paris: Organization for Economic Cooperation and Development/International Transport Forum. Available at http://dx.doi.org/10.1787/9789282107782-en.

Olken, Benjamin. 2007. Monitoring Corruption: Evidence from a Field Experiment in Indonesia. *Journal of Political Economy* 115, no. 2: 200–49.

Ostry, Jonathan D., Andrew Berg, and Charalambos G. Tsangarides. 2014. *Redistribution, Inequality, and Growth*. IMF Staff Discussion Note 14/12. Washington: International Monetary Fund.

Oxfam. 2016. *An Economy for the 1 Percent*. Briefing Paper 210. Oxford, UK.

Pampel, Fred. 2010. Divergent Patterns of Smoking across High-Income Nations. In *International Differences in Mortality at Older Ages*. Washington: National Academies Press.

Piketty, Thomas. 2014. *Capital in the Twenty-First Century*. Cambridge, MA: Harvard University Press.

Pinkovskiy, Maxim, and Xavier Sala-i-Martín. 2010. *African Poverty Is Falling...Much Faster than You Think!* NBER Working Paper 15775. Cambridge, MA: National Bureau of Economic Research.

Pissarides, Christopher A., and Guglielmo Weber. 1989. An Expenditure-Based Estimate of Britain's Black Economy. *Journal of Public Economics* 39, no. 1: 17–32.

Pritchett, Lant, and Lawrence H. Summers. 2014. *Asiaphoria Meets Regression to the Mean*. NBER Working Paper 20573. Cambridge, MA: National Bureau of Economic Research.

Ravallion, Martin. 2012. Why Don't We See Poverty Convergence? *American Economic Review* 102, no. 1: 504–23.

Ravallion, Martin, and Shaohua Chen. 1997. What Can the Survey Data Tell Us about Recent Changes in Distribution and Poverty? *World Bank Economic Review* 11, no. 2: 357–82.

Rawls, John. 1999. *The Law of Peoples*. Cambridge, MA: Harvard University Press.

Risse, Mathias. 2006. What to Say about the State. *Social Theory and Practice* 32: 671–98.

Rome, Adam. 2015. The Launch of Spaceship Earth. *Nature* 527: 443–45.

Rosenstein-Rodan, Paul N. 1943. Problems of Industrialisation of Eastern and South-Eastern Europe. *The Economic Journal* 53, no. 210/211: 202–11.

Sala-i-Martín, Xavier. 2006. The World Distribution of Income: Falling Poverty and...Convergence, Period. *Quarterly Journal of Economics* 121, no. 2: 351–97.

Sandel, Michael J. 2009. *Justice: What's the Right Thing to Do?* New York: Farrar, Straus and Giroux.

Sangiovanni, Andrea. 2007. Global Justice, Reciprocity, and the State. *Philosophy and Public Affairs* 35: 3–39.

Schiermeier, Quirin. 2015. China's Birth Rate Won't Be Dramatically Affected by End of One-Child Policy. *Nature* (October 29). Available at www.nature.com/news/china-s-birth-rate-won-t-be-dramatically-affected-by-end-of-one-child-policy-1.18687.

Schneider, Friedrich, and Dominik H. Enste. 2013. *The Shadow Economy: An International Survey*. Cambridge: Cambridge University Press.

Schuetze, Herb J. 2002. Profiles of Tax Noncompliance among Self-Employed in Canada: 1969–1992. *Canadian Public Policy* 28, no. 2: 219–37.

Schultz, T. Paul. 1998. Inequality in the Distribution of Personal Income in the World: How It Is Changing and Why. *Journal of Population Economics* 11, no. 3: 307–44.

Solt, Frederick. 2014. *The Standardized World Income Inequality Database*. Working Paper, Department of Political Science, University of Iowa, Iowa City. Available at http://myweb.uiowa.edu/fsolt/papers/Solt2014.pdf.

Summers, Lawrence H. 2016. The Age of Secular Stagnation: What It Is and What to Do About It. *Foreign Affairs* (March/April). Available at www.foreignaffairs.com/articles/united-states/2016-02-15/age-secular-stagnation.

Székely, M., and M. Hilgert. 1999. *What's Behind the Inequality We Measure? An Investigation Using Latin American Data*. Research Department Working Paper. Washington: Inter-American Development Bank.

United Nations. 2008. *Non-Observed Economy in National Accounts: Survey of Country Practices*. New York.

United Nations. 2015. *World Population Prospects: The 2015 Revision, Key Findings and Advance Tables*. Working Paper ESA/P/WP.241. New York: Department of Economic and Social Affairs, Population Division.

Warner, Andrew M. 2014. *Public Investment as an Engine of Growth*. IMF Working Paper 14/148. Washington: International Monetary Fund.

Weisman, Steven R. 2015. *The Great Tradeoff: Confronting Moral Conflicts in the Era of Globalization*. Washington: Peterson Institute for International Economics.

World Bank. 2015. *The Worldwide Governance Indicators, 2015 Update*. Available at www.govindicators.org.

World Bank and OECD (Organization for Economic Cooperation and Development). 2015. *Project Checklist for Public-Private Partnerships*. Washington.

World Bank Group. 2016. *Global Monitoring Report 2015/2016: Development Goals in an Era of Demographic Change*. Washington.

World Bank Group and OECD (Organization for Economic Cooperation and Development). 2015. Project Checklist for Public-Private Partnerships. Available at www.oecd.org/daf/fin/financial-markets/WBG-OECD-Checklist-for-PPP-Projects.pdf.

World Economic Forum. 2015. *Global Competitiveness Report 2015–16*. Geneva.

Index

Other Publications from the
PETERSON INSTITUTE FOR INTERNATIONAL ECONOMICS

POLICY ANALYSES IN INTERNATIONAL ECONOMICS SERIES

* = out of print

Economic Consequences of Soviet Disintegration* John Williamson, ed.
May 1993 ISBN 0-88132-190-7

Reconcilable Differences? United States-Japan Economic Conflict* C. Fred Bergsten and Marcus Noland
June 1993 ISBN 0-88132-129-X

Does Foreign Exchange Intervention Work? Kathryn M. Dominguez and Jeffrey A. Frankel
September 1993 ISBN 0-88132-104-4

Sizing Up U.S. Export Disincentives* J. David Richardson
September 1993 ISBN 0-88132-107-9

NAFTA: An Assessment* Gary Clyde Hufbauer and Jeffrey J. Schott, *rev. ed.*
October 1993 ISBN 0-88132-199-0

Adjusting to Volatile Energy Prices Philip K. Verleger, Jr.
November 1993 ISBN 0-88132-069-2

The Political Economy of Policy Reform John Williamson, ed.
January 1994 ISBN 0-88132-195-8

Measuring the Costs of Protection in the United States Gary Clyde Hufbauer and Kimberly Ann Elliott
January 1994 ISBN 0-88132-108-7

The Dynamics of Korean Economic Development* Cho Soon
March 1994 ISBN 0-88132-162-1

Reviving the European Union* C. Randall Henning, Eduard Hochreiter, and Gary Clyde Hufbauer, eds.
April 1994 ISBN 0-88132-208-3

China in the World Economy Nicholas R. Lardy
April 1994 ISBN 0-88132-200-8

Greening the GATT: Trade, Environment, and the Future Daniel C. Esty
July 1994 ISBN 0-88132-205-9

Western Hemisphere Economic Integration* Gary Clyde Hufbauer and Jeffrey J. Schott
July 1994 ISBN 0-88132-159-1

Currencies and Politics in the United States, Germany, and Japan C. Randall Henning
September 1994 ISBN 0-88132-127-3

Estimating Equilibrium Exchange Rates John Williamson, ed.
September 1994 ISBN 0-88132-076-5

Managing the World Economy: Fifty Years after Bretton Woods Peter B. Kenen, ed.
September 1994 ISBN 0-88132-212-1

Trade Liberalization and International Institutions* Jeffrey J. Schott
September 1994 ISBN 978-0-88132-3

Reciprocity and Retaliation in U.S. Trade Policy* Thomas O. Bayard and Kimberly Ann Elliott
September 1994 ISBN 0-88132-084-6

The Uruguay Round: An Assessment* Jeffrey J. Schott, assisted by Johanna Buurman
November 1994 ISBN 0-88132-206-7

Measuring the Costs of Protection in Japan* Yoko Sazanami, Shujiro Urata, and Hiroki Kawai
January 1995 ISBN 0-88132-211-3

Foreign Direct Investment in the United States, 3d ed. Edward M. Graham and Paul R. Krugman
January 1995 ISBN 0-88132-204-0

The Political Economy of Korea-United States Cooperation* C. Fred Bergsten and Il SaKong, eds.
February 1995 ISBN 0-88132-213-X

International Debt Reexamined* William R. Cline
February 1995 ISBN 0-88132-083-8

American Trade Politics, 3d ed. I. M. Destler
April 1995 ISBN 0-88132-215-6

Managing Official Export Credits: The Quest for a Global Regime* John E. Ray
July 1995 ISBN 0-88132-207-5

Asia Pacific Fusion: Japan's Role in APEC Yoichi Funabashi
October 1995 ISBN 0-88132-224-5

Korea-United States Cooperation in the New World Order* C. Fred Bergsten and Il SaKong, eds.
February 1996 ISBN 0-88132-226-1

Why Exports Really Matter!* ISBN 0-88132-221-0
Why Exports Matter More!* ISBN 0-88132-229-6
J. David Richardson and Karin Rindal
July 1995; February 1996

Global Corporations and National Governments Edward M. Graham
May 1996 ISBN 0-88132-111-7

Global Economic Leadership and the Group of Seven C. Fred Bergsten and C. Randall Henning
May 1996 ISBN 0-88132-218-0

The Trading System after the Uruguay Round* John Whalley and Colleen Hamilton
July 1996 ISBN 0-88132-131-1

Private Capital Flows to Emerging Markets after the Mexican Crisis* Guillermo A. Calvo, Morris Goldstein, and Eduard Hochreiter
September 1996 ISBN 0-88132-232-6

The Crawling Band as an Exchange Rate Regime: Lessons from Chile, Colombia, and Israel John Williamson
September 1996 ISBN 0-88132-231-8

Flying High: Liberalizing Civil Aviation in the Asia Pacific* Gary Clyde Hufbauer and Christopher Findlay
November 1996 ISBN 0-88132-227-X

Measuring the Costs of Visible Protection in Korea* Namdoo Kim
November 1996 ISBN 0-88132-236-9

The World Trading System: Challenges Ahead Jeffrey J. Schott
December 1996 ISBN 0-88132-235-0

Has Globalization Gone Too Far? Dani Rodrik
March 1997 ISBN paper 0-88132-241-5

Korea-United States Economic Relationship* C. Fred Bergsten and Il SaKong, eds.
March 1997 ISBN 0-88132-240-7

Summitry in the Americas: A Progress Report* Richard E. Feinberg
April 1997 ISBN 0-88132-242-3

Corruption and the Global Economy Kimberly Ann Elliott
June 1997 ISBN 0-88132-233-4

Regional Trading Blocs in the World Economic System Jeffrey A. Frankel
October 1997 ISBN 0-88132-202-4

Sustaining the Asia Pacific Miracle: Environmental Protection and Economic Integration Andre Dua and Daniel C. Esty
October 1997 ISBN 0-88132-250-4

Can Labor Standards Improve under
Globalization?   Kimberly Ann Elliott and
Richard B. Freeman
June 2003   ISBN 0-88132-332-2
Crimes and Punishments? Retaliation under the
WTO   Robert Z. Lawrence
October 2003   ISBN 0-88132-359-4
Inflation Targeting in the World Economy
Edwin M. Truman
October 2003   ISBN 0-88132-345-4
Foreign Direct Investment and Tax Competition
John H. Mutti
November 2003   ISBN 0-88132-352-7
Has Globalization Gone Far Enough? The Costs
of Fragmented Markets   Scott C. Bradford and
Robert Z. Lawrence
February 2004   ISBN 0-88132-349-7
Food Regulation and Trade: Toward a Safe and
Open Global System   Tim Josling, Donna Roberts,
and David Orden
March 2004   ISBN 0-88132-346-2
Controlling Currency Mismatches in Emerging
Markets   Morris Goldstein and Philip Turner
April 2004   ISBN 0-88132-360-8
Free Trade Agreements: US Strategies and
Priorities   Jeffrey J. Schott, ed.
April 2004   ISBN 0-88132-361-6
Trade Policy and Global Poverty
William R. Cline
June 2004   ISBN 0-88132-365-9
Bailouts or Bail-ins? Responding to Financial
Crises in Emerging Economies   Nouriel Roubini
and Brad Setser
August 2004   ISBN 0-88132-371-3
Transforming the European Economy
Martin Neil Baily and Jacob Funk Kirkegaard
September 2004   ISBN 0-88132-343-8
Getting Aid To Work: Politics, Policies and
Incentives For Poor Countries*
Nicolas Van De Walle
Septbember 2004   ISBN 0-88132-379-9
Chasing Dirty Money: The Fight Against Money
Laundering   Peter Reuter and Edwin M. Truman
November 2004   ISBN 0-88132-370-5
The United States and the World Economy:
Foreign Economic Policy for the Next Decade
C. Fred Bergsten
January 2005   ISBN 0-88132-380-2
Does Foreign Direct Investment Promote
Development?   Theodore H. Moran,
Edward M. Graham, and Magnus Blomström, eds.
April 2005   ISBN 0-88132-381-0
American Trade Politics, 4th ed.   I. M. Destler
June 2005   ISBN 0-88132-382-9
Shell Global Scenarios to 2025: The Future
Business Environment: Trends, Trade-offs and
Choices*
June 2005   ISBN 0-88132-383-7
Why Does Immigration Divide America? Public
Finance and Political Opposition to Open
Borders   Gordon H. Hanson
August 2005   ISBN 0-88132-400-0
Reforming the US Corporate Tax
Gary Clyde Hufbauer and Paul L. E. Grieco
September 2005   ISBN 0-88132-384-5

The United States as a Debtor Nation
William R. Cline
September 2005   ISBN 0-88132-399-3
NAFTA Revisited: Achievements and Challenges
Gary Clyde Hufbauer and Jeffrey J. Schott, assisted
by Paul L. E. Grieco and Yee Wong
October 2005   ISBN 0-88132-334-9
US National Security and Foreign Direct
Investment   Edward M. Graham and
David M. Marchick
May 2006   ISBN 978-0-88132-391-7
Accelerating the Globalization of America: The
Role for Information Technology
Catherine L. Mann, assisted by Jacob Funk
Kirkegaard
June 2006   ISBN 978-0-88132-390-0
Delivering on Doha: Farm Trade and the Poor
Kimberly Ann Elliott
July 2006   ISBN 978-0-88132-392-4
Case Studies in US Trade Negotiation, Vol. 1:
Making the Rules   Charan Devereaux,
Robert Z. Lawrence, and Michael Watkins
September 2006   ISBN 978-0-88132-362-7
Case Studies in US Trade Negotiation, Vol. 2:
Resolving Disputes   Charan Devereaux,
Robert Z. Lawrence, and Michael Watkins
September 2006   ISBN 978-0-88132-363-2
C. Fred Bergsten and the World Economy
Michael Mussa, ed.
December 2006   ISBN 978-0-88132-397-9
Working Papers, Volume I   Peterson Institute
December 2006   ISBN 978-0-88132-388-7
The Arab Economies in a Changing World
Marcus Noland and Howard Pack
April 2007   ISBN 978-0-88132-393-1
Working Papers, Volume II Peterson Institute
April 2007   ISBN 978-0-88132-404-4
Global Warming and Agriculture: Impact
Estimates by Country   William R. Cline
July 2007   ISBN 978-0-88132-403-7
US Taxation of Foreign Income
Gary Clyde Hufbauer and Ariel Assa
October 2007   ISBN 978-0-88132-405-1
Russia's Capitalist Revolution: Why Market
Reform Succeeded and Democracy Failed
Anders Åslund
October 2007   ISBN 978-0-88132-409-9
Economic Sanctions Reconsidered, 3d ed.
Gary Clyde Hufbauer, Jeffrey J. Schott, Kimberly
Ann Elliott, and Barbara Oegg
November 2007
          ISBN hardcover 978-0-88132-407-5
          ISBN hardcover/CD-ROM 978-0-88132-408-2
Debating China's Exchange Rate Policy
Morris Goldstein and Nicholas R. Lardy, eds.
April 2008   ISBN 978-0-88132-415-0
Leveling the Carbon Playing Field: International
Competition and US Climate Policy Design
Trevor Houser, Rob Bradley, Britt Childs, Jacob
Werksman, and Robert Heilmayr
May 2008   ISBN 978-0-88132-420-4
Accountability and Oversight of US Exchange
Rate Policy   C. Randall Henning
June 2008   ISBN 978-0-88132-419-8

BOOKS IN PROGRESS

Sales Representatives

In Asia, North America, and South America

Perseus Distribution
210 American Drive
Jackson, TN 38301
orderentry@perseusbooks.com

Tel. (800) 343-4499
Fax (800) 351-5073
Email: cup_book@columbia.edu

Secure online ordering is available on the CUP website at: www.cup.columbia.edu

In Africa, Europe, the Middle East, South Africa, South Asias, and the United States

Columbia University Press
c/o Wiley European Distribution Centre
New Era Estate
Oldlands Way, Bognor Regis
West Sussex PO22 9NQ

Tel. (1243) 843-291
Fax (1243) 843-296
Email: customer@wiley.com

(Delivery via Wiley Distribution Services Ltd., or you may collect your order by prior arrangement)

United States and Canada Sales and Publicity Representatives

Brad Hebel, Director of Sales and Marketing
61 West 62nd Street
New York, NY 10023

Tel. (212) 459-0600, ext. 7130
Fax (212) 459-3678
Email: bh2106@columbia.edu

Columbia University Sales Consortium Manager and Souther US

Catherine Hobbs

Tel. (804) 690-8529
Fax (434) 589-3411
Email: catherinehobbs@earthlink.net

Northeast US and Eastern Canada

Conor Broughan

Tel. (917) 826-7676
Email: cb2476@columbia.edu

Midwest US and Central Canada

Kevin Kurtz

Tel. (773) 316-1116
Fax (773) 489-2941
Email: kkurtz5@earthlink.net

Western US and Western Canada

William Gawronski

Tel. (310) 488-9059
Fax (310) 832-4717
Email: wgawronski@earthlink.net

United Kingdom and Europe

The University Press Group Ltd.
Lois Edwards
LEC 1, New Era Estate
Oldlands Way, Bognor Regis
PO22 9NQ England

Tel. 44 (1243) 842-165
Fax 44 (1243) 842-167
Email: lois@upguk.com

Ben Mitchell
U.K. Sales Manager
62 Fairford House
Kennington Lane
London SE11 4HR England

Tel. (44) 776-691-3593
Email: ben.mitchell.upg@gmail.com

Andrew Brewer
Managing Director
57 Cobnar Road
Sheffield S8 8QA England

Tel. (44) 114-274-0129
Mobile (44) 796-703-1856
Email: andrew.brewer@virgin.net

Middle East and Africa

Andrew Brewer
Managing Director
57 Cobnar Road
Sheffield S8 8QA England

Tel. (44) 114-274-0129
Mobile (44) 796-703-1856
Email: andrew.brewer@virgin.net

Asia

Brad Hebel
61 West 62nd Street
New York, NY 10023

Tel. (212) 459-0600, ext. 7130
Fax (212) 459-3678
Email: bh2106@columbia.edu